Traditional Korean Legal Attitudes

A publication of the
Center for Korean Studies
Institute of East Asian Studies
University of California
Berkeley, California 94720

The Korea Research Monograph Series of the Center for Korean Studies is one of three monograph series published by the Institute of East Asian Studies. The other two are the Japan Research Monograph Series of the Center for Japanese Studies, and the China Research Monograph Series of the Center for Chinese Studies.

Correspondence may be sent to:
Director of Publications
Institute of East Asian Studies
University of California
Berkeley, California 94720

KORREA RESEARCH MONOGRAPH 2

INSTITUTE OF EAST ASIAN STUDIES
UNIVERSITY OF CALIFORNIA · BERKELEY
CENTER FOR KOREAN STUDIES

Traditional Korean Legal Attitudes

BONG DUCK CHUN
WILLIAM SHAW
DAI-KWON CHOI

ISBN 0-912966-30-0
Library of Congress Catalog Number 80-620036
Printed in the United States of America
$8.00

Contents

Legal Attitudes of the Late Yi Dynasty 1

Bong Duck Chun

Social and Intellectual Aspects of Traditional Korean Law, 1392–1910 15

William Shaw

The Development of Law and Legal Institutions in Korea 54

Dai-Kwon Choi

Preface

In March 1979 the Institute of East Asian Studies sponsored a four-day conference on Korean legal institutions and attitudes. In several respects it was a pioneer venture. Opportunities for close intellectual collaboration between American and Korean scholars have been scarce, notwithstanding decades of close economic and political relationships between our two countries. It is true, of course, that a great many Korean intellectuals have studied in the United States, and equally true that a growing number of American scholars have visited Korea—despite the relatively few American specialists in this field. Yet, to bring American and Korean scholarship to bear on a common topic, even one as broad as that set forth above, is relatively rare.

With the three essays presented here, we issue the first of what will be three monographs drawn from the papers presented at the conference. As the reader will note, these papers deal essentially with the background of Korean legal institutions and values, setting forth selected aspects of the subject. Our three specialists—Dr. Bong Duck Chun, Dr. William Shaw, and Professor Dai-Kwon Choi—have presented us with suggestive insights into subjects seldom explored by American scholars. We hope that this will represent the beginning of cooperative scholarship bringing together American and Korean scholars on many subjects of mutual interest.

Robert A. Scalapino
Director, Institute of
East Asian Studies

Legal Principles and Values of the Late Yi Dynasty

Bong Duck Chun*

To understand the legal foundations of traditional Korean society, it is essential to be acquainted with the central principles of Confucianism, and the manner in which these principles underwrote the sociopolitical order of Korea. We may define the Korean polity as authoritarianism with some unique features loosely encompassed in the term "oriental despotism."[1]

KOREAN TRADITIONAL VALUES

In traditional Korea, political power was concentrated in the person of the king, with this concentration made possible by the all-inclusive appointment powers of the monarch. Every official, whether at the center or in the provinces, held power at the pleasure of the king. All authority flowed from his person. Yet we are immediately confronted with a paradox. Rarely did the monarch exercise the unlimited power implicit in his office. In fact, most kings during the Yi dynasty were physically weak or very young when they came to the throne. Nor were they highly educated. Their advent to office came through power struggles among branches of

---

*A note on Romanization: The Reischauer-McCune method is generally used throughout; however, to avoid confusion this system was not applied to names of authors whose works have been published in English language journals and Romanized in some other fashion. Each author's preference for Romanizing his own name has been respected.

[1] Han U-gŭn, *The History of Korea*, trans. Lee Kyung-sik, ed. Grafton K. Mintz (Seoul: Ul-Yu Publishing Co., 1970), p. 203.

the royal family and high officials. Yi-dynasty monarchs thus exercised power only with and through the bureaucracy, as in traditional China.

Since the king could not legitimize his authority on the basis of his personal achievements or abilities, another route had to be followed: that of the familiar "mandate of heaven." At the heart of Confucian doctrine lay the concept that the monarch was a representative of heaven, governing his people in accordance with heaven's principles. From this concept stemmed the traditional theories of legitimacy and monarchical responsibility. A king pursuing the mandate of heaven heeded the interests of the people because "heaven sees as my people see; heaven hears as my people hear."[2] In essence, the will of heaven was embodied in the will of the people, and righteous government could only be realized if the monarch won the hearts of the people. Needless to say, this did not lead to public participation in governing, but, in some settings, it did serve to justify rebellion, and it proved to be a powerful weapon in the hands of the officials because it was they who could interpret the public will.

To achieve the ancient Confucian ideal of "the kingly way," monarchs underwent a rigorous educational program akin in some respects to the training required of those entering religious orders in the West. The classical injunction was to cultivate oneself in preparation for ruling a family, and to rule a family in preparation for governing the state and leading the country peacefully.[3] The monarch was supposed to achieve self-perfection through the constant pursuit of knowledge and the cultivation of virtue. He was to aim at becoming like the ancient Chinese emperors Yao and Shun, idealized figures of perfect virtue and wisdom. Similarly, the models for scholar-officials were Confucius and Mencius.

The king's duties in traditional Korea were essentially twofold: first, to discern the true conditions pertaining to his subjects and to participate in policy-making discussions and decisions; second, to master the Confucian doctrines. The former task was undertaken through consultation with the three chief ministers of the State Council, the ministers of the Six Boards, and other high-ranking officials. It also required taking advice from the two boards of censors and other officials, including special counselors, as well as meeting periodically with the secretaries of the Six Boards.[4] The second obligation was fulfilled by regularly attending lectures given by royal tutors three times a day. By these means, serving as both advisers and instructors, the officials who surrounded the king were

---

[2]James Legge, trans. and ed., *The Chinese Classics* (Hong Kong: Hong Kong University Press, 1970), II:357.

[3]Ibid., I:357.

[4]The six ministries are: Personnel Affairs, Revenues, Rituals, Military Affairs, Criminal Affairs, and Public Works.

in a strong position to exercise restraints on and provide direction to monarchical power.

Scholarly controversy has long existed over the question whether the Yi dynasty should be regarded as a centralized authoritarian system of a special type or a system akin to the West European style of absolutism.[5] It is my view that to identify the Yi dynasty with the type of centralized monarchical absolutism that emerged in Europe is in error. European absolutism in its early modern form came into being only after the feudal system had been toppled and in the course of national integration. Indeed, it was premised on the latter development. Yet during the Yi dynasty, before the 1894–1895 reforms, there was no such national integration in political terms. Korea was a society whose people, to borrow Sun Yat-sen's characterization of the Chinese, "were like loose grains of sand."[6]

Although central and local administrative organs were under the direct control of the king, relations among central offices and between central and local authorities were not systematically regulated. The officials of each organ were given ranks appropriate to their function and status, but neither the scope of their authority nor their relations with other offices were governed by rational bureaucratic criteria, and that also applied to appointment, dismissal, and rotation in office. Even with respect to salaries and administrative expenses, no fixed regulations existed. Rather than the centralized, routinized administrative structure that emerged in the West, the traditional Korean political system was a highly personalized, despotic system based on a concentration of power at the top, but with a looseness of structure that resulted in pseudo-centralization in fact.

To understand the basic nature of the Korean political system, one must turn to the family prototype. In traditional Korea as in China, the model for societal politics was the patriarchal family. Patriarchalism here refers to a household system in which a family head or patriarch, wife, concubines, and various other family members resided. Each such household comprised a kinship-based body, with fixed functional and status divisions, supposedly operating efficiently and harmoniously, abiding by an "ethics of good will." Confucianism set an ideal of four generations living under one roof. Each family member was required to play his or her assigned role under the leadership and protection of the patriarch. To give precedence to one's own interest over the interests of the fam-

[5] Yi Tal-sun, "The Absolutism of Yi Dynasty," *The Korean Political Science Review*, 6 (1972):33.

[6] Sun Yat-sen, *San Min Chu I* [The Three Principles of the People], trans. Frank W. Price, ed. L. T. Chen (Chungking: Institute of Pacific Relations, 1943), pp. 363–407.

ily was considered shameful. In the ideology fostered by the traditional Korean life-style, there was no room for individualism.

In principle, the authority of the family head was sacred and absolute. He held the power of life or death over all family members. Filial piety–the respect of the younger for the older–was the basis for the hierarchical family structure, and filial piety represented a value, religious in character, derived from the view of patriarchal authority as sacred. If one divides authority along Weberian lines into authoritarian-charismatic and modern-legal, the Yi-dynasty family system clearly belonged to the former, with obedience to the patriarch held to be absolute and unconditional.[7] Father symbolized heaven to son; husband bore the same symbolism to wife.[8] In the words of the Confucianist Yi Hwang (1501–1570), "There are not two suns in the sky, nor two kings over the people, nor two heads of a family, nor two principal mourners at a funeral."[9]

Confucianism served as a political ideology connecting family and state. The word for "state" came from two Chinese characters meaning "country" and "family." Throughout the Confucian world, the state was seen as the family writ large, and the family was regarded as the model for the state. The preface to the fifteenth-century dynastic code made the latter view explicit: "The family is transformed into the state." King and father were interchangeable concepts, as were people and children. Filial piety was thus transmuted directly into the principle of loyalty between subject and monarch. Indeed, loyalty and filial piety were often linked in a single term, *ch'unghyo*, as the following quotation from the *Lü shih Ch'un ch'iu* indicates: "He who serves his parents with filial piety (*ch'unghyo*) will serve his prince with loyalty (*ch'unghyo*); he who serves his prince with disloyalty will not serve his parents with filial piety."

In traditional Korea as in China, Confucianism underwrote a strongly status-conscious society. The emphasis upon *ch'ŏnha t'aep'yŏng* (great peace under heaven) referred to the need for people to keep their proper position in society. Korea lived by the maxim of the Duke of Ch'i: "There is government when the prince acts as prince, and the minister acts as minister; [there is government] when the father acts as father, and the son acts as son."[10] As in China, status distinction (*myŏngbun*) was vital to the preservation of order, with a strict differentiation being made between the *yangban* (government office holders) and other classes. Moral princi-

---

[7] Max Weber, *Economy and Society*, trans. Ephraim Fitschoff et al., ed. Guenther Roth and Claus Wittich (New York: Bedminster Press, 1968), pp. 227–241.

[8] *Chosŏn Wangjo Sillok* [Royal Records of the Yi Dynasty], ed. Kuksa P'yŏnch'an Wiwonhoe (Seoul: Kuksa Pyŏnch'an Wiwonhoe, 1955), III:579.

[9] Yi Hwang, *T'oegyejip* (Seoul: Minjok Munhwa Ch'ujinhoe, 1968), I:101.

[10] Legge, *The Chinese Classics*, I:256.

ples were regarded as applying primarily to "the great men and officials," governing the manner in which the upper class should relate to both monarch and the lower classes. For the latter, emulation would follow if their superior set the proper standards. As Confucius wrote: "The relation between superiors and inferiors is like that between the wind and the grass."[11]

Inequality was the rule not merely between noble and commoner but also between male and female, and between those engaged in intellectual pursuits and those committed to manual labor. Universally accepted was Mencius' prescription: "Those who work with their minds govern others; those who labor with their physical strength are governed by others. Those who are governed by others support themselves; those who govern others are supported by those whom they govern. This is a principle which is universally recognized."[12]

The traditional social order during the Yi dynasty was virtually identical with that of China, being defined in terms of the "five human relationships" (*oryun*). Three of these relationships, those between sovereign and minister, father and son, and husband and wife, were designated the "three bonds" (*samgang*). The relation between elder and younger, and that between friends, represented the remaining two.[13] Thus political and familial relationships constituted an unbreakable continuum, with each relationship underwritten by the same basic values. In these relationships, no concept was more important than that of benevolence (*jen*). Yet benevolence, being derivative from, and rooted in, filial piety, could not extend beyond the prescribed five relationships. Thus, the hostility toward strangers, those lacking kinship ties and, conversely, the extensive practice of nepotism within governing circles reflect the negative aspects of the Confucian impact upon those societies partaking of Sinic culture, aspects that have projected themselves into the contemporary era.

To understand the traditional social order, however, it is essential to understand the role and status of the *yangban* class. The *yangban* was composed of two groups: civil officials and military officers who held official rank. Every official, civil or military, was appointed by the king, and given stipendiary lands according to his position. Persons who had played a special role in helping a king against rivals were given special royal grants of land. These lands were inherited by the children of the original grantees even after they had departed from office. In essence, the *yangban* class had its social base in office holding, its economic base in the land grants accompanying office. The Korean *yangban* system was dif-

[11] Ibid., p. 259.

[12] Ibid., II:249–250.

[13] Ibid., p. 252.

ferent from the nobility of western Europe in which status change was rare. Upward mobility from the lower classes to the *yangban* class was reasonably high, since a lower-class family could become a *yangban* family when a family member was appointed to a high-ranking position. Naturally, a *yangban* family sought to occupy high-ranking offices from generation to generation so as to retain its status. Yet when such a family had no member in office for an extended time, it was forced to depart for the countryside, away from the center of power, and to live like commoners.

As has been indicated, the *yangban* were at root an office-holding class, encompassing a wide range of individuals–civil and military incumbents, former officials and their families. To hold office meant not only holding power oneself but having the opportunity to secure wealth and power for one's entire family. *Yangban* families were also landlords, drawing income from peasant tenants by the right to collect taxes. They were exempt from military and other compulsory public services and from various taxes. A centrally controlled tax system did not exist during the Yi era. Tax collection was in the hands of local officials who often were given latitude to manipulate taxes and in the process acquire great wealth. *Yangban* status therefore became a synonym for wealth.[14]

Yi society was in essence a society of and for the *yangban*. Social contact between *yangban* and commoners was carefully circumscribed and strictly regulated, as were the activities of the *yangban* themselves. When a *yangban* left his home, his clothing and hat had to be carefully arranged, and he was accompanied by a number of slaves (according to his rank), some of whom supported his arms as he walked.[15] In economic transactions, contracts and similar matters, agreements were generally concluded in the name of the *yangban*'s household slaves in accordance with the injunction of the *Analects* that "the superior man thinks of virtue."[16] The intention was to avoid the "unethical activities" of "small men," at least in form. The latter were regarded as being preoccupied with economic concerns such as land and profits. The *yangban* (guaranteed an eminently satisfactory economic base) were supposedly above these "vulgar" matters, dedicated to the acquisition of virtue and righteousness through study and contemplation. Traditional Korean Confucianism underwrote the cultivation of a true leisure class, one holding labor in contempt as the proper business of the mean man. This view stood in striking contrast to the Protestant ethic with its commitment to labor as a

---

[14] Han, *The History of Korea*, p. 248.

[15] Pŏpchech'ŏ, trans. and ed., *Kyŏngguk Taejŏn* [The Grand Code of Yi Dynasty, 1485] (Seoul: Pŏpchech'ŏ, 1962), II:192.

[16] Legge, *The Chinese Classics*, I:168.

"calling" from God, hence endowed with high spiritual value, and suggests the dimensions of the revolution later borne by the missionary intrusion into Korea.

As the deep impact of Confucianism suggests, the *yangban*, as Korea's scholar-gentry class, paid homage to China, accepting the view that their culture was derivative from and inferior to that of the Central Kingdom. One manifestation of respect for China was to advocate the expulsion of barbarians, namely, all foreign intruders other than the Chinese. Through a policy of national isolation, the *yangban* believed that they were defending Confucian orthodoxy, driving away those who would defile traditional values. In 1866, for example, toward the end of the Yi dynasty, the regent T'aewŏn-gun, father of King Kojong, ordered that stone markers with the following inscription be placed throughout Korea: "When foreign barbarians invade, if we do not fight, there will be peace; yet he who urges such a peace sells out his country."[17]

This inscription was symbolic of the isolationist mood and policies of the late nineteenth century. The implacable conservatism of the *yangban* class, involving as it did an unswerving support for the status quo in all of its aspects and a rejection of the new socioeconomic and political-legal ideas that were beginning to sweep in from the external world, blocked all possibilities of reform. Thus, the *yangban* bureaucratic class must be held responsible for the trauma that was to follow—progressive internal weakness and decay, chaos followed by colonization.

THE ROLE OF LAW

Traditional Korean legal attitudes and practices cannot be understood without reference to the sociopolitical context sketched briefly above. We now turn to the role of law under the Yi dynasty.

In the Yi period, royal edicts having the force of law were termed *kyo* (instructions). *Hagyo* was the process of sending down the king's edicts to the lower-level offices of the government, and *sugyo* (received instructions or edicts) were the administrative instructions of the king. From the viewpoint of the government agency concerned, they were equivalent to law in the modern sense.

Laws could also be made by the king's approving of proposals submitted by individual ministers or government officials. These laws were known as *sup'an* (received decisions). Until 1404, government agencies apparently were able to legislate even without royal authority. However, in that year the Board of Rites recommended that all proposed legislation be discussed by the State Council and approved or rejected by the king:

---

[17] Han, *The History of Korea*, p. 368.

> In the establishment of law, only those laws which may be expected to last indefinitely without causing any subsequent difficulties are fully worthy of the name. The various government offices like to make laws; but things have reached the point where the agencies concerned cannot keep all the laws and there are many problems. Henceforward when laws are made, the draft proposals should be fully deliberated at the State Council and put into force only after receiving the approval of the king (*sup'an*).[18]

Despite this recommendation, both types of law-making continued, although the word *sup'an* was dropped from use in the early fifteenth century and only *sugyo* used for all new laws, whether of royal or bureaucratic origin.[19]

The *Kyŏngje yukchŏn* (Six Codes for Governing the Country) of 1397, promulgated by King T'aejo, and its later supplements such as the *Sok yukchŏn* (Supplementary Six Codes) were compilations of the basic laws considered suitable for continued use, and they comprised both types of law mentioned above. Through these and subsequent compilations, the "received edicts" on file were reviewed and edited; provisional and inoperative ones were discarded. The compilations were in six sections because the work took place initially at each of the six boards of government: Personnel, Revenue, Rites, War, Punishments, and Public Works.

The early dynastic Six Codes compilations have not survived. The earliest extant Yi-dynasty code is the *Kyŏngguk taejŏn* (Great Code for Governing the Country), compiled in 1484 during Sŏngjong's reign and put into effect the following year. The last code of the Yi dynasty, the *Taejŏn hoet'ong* (Great Code and Collected Supplements) was compiled in 1865.

As indicated, the compilation of law codes was intended to select only those "received edicts" suitable for continued use. However, early Yi kings found it difficult to codify edicts that implied the abrogation of earlier codified law. When T'aejong (r. 1400–1418) found contradictions between T'aejo's code and his own supplementary codification, he ordered the editors to omit edicts contradicting the original code of King T'aejo. His order reads: "All received edicts must follow the original *Kyŏngje yukchŏn*. In compiling the supplementary Six Codes, those laws contradicting the original code are to be deleted."[20] Thus T'aejong's attempt to unify the legal system was based on the original codification of T'aejo and indeed T'aejong's own codification was titled simply the "Supplementary Six Codes." This principle of respecting earlier law—

[18] *Chosŏn Wangjo Sillok*, I:313.

[19] Ibid., II:680.

[20] Ibid., p. 81.

contrary to the modern concept of legislation—was largely observed in later edict compilations as well.

To King Sejo, who began the compilation of the *Kyŏngguk taejŏn*, and King Sŏngjong who completed this work, the *Kyŏngguk taejŏn* was thought of as the repository of the "established enactments of the royal ancestors." The preface, written by Sŏ Kŏ-jŏng, made this view explicit: "Henceforward, if our kings, who are descended from sages and divinities, hold to and execute the established enactments of their royal ancestors, the glory of our country's civilized government will be worthy of comparison with that of ancient Chou."

The fact that the last code of law of the Yi dynasty, the *Taejŏn hoet'ong*, preserves intact those provisions of the *Kyŏngguk taejŏn* that had continued to be effective as positive law, illustrates how firmly the principle of retaining the ancestors' law was established. It also illustrates the impact on the Yi dynasty of the traditional Confucian view, which regarded the time of Yao and Shun unconditionally as a golden age—the past as better than the present, and the ancestral law as *gutes altes Recht* (good ancient law). In the official Yi-dynasty view, the culture and legal systems were complete; the only acceptable improvement, a return to the earlier era. Accordingly, the legal thought of the Yi dynasty could not accept the Western principle that "a later statute nullifies the effect of a prior one." The contrary principle was so strong that new laws were effective only when they did not conflict with the old laws. Apart from the difficulties that this situation created in the legal sphere, it reinforced the people's conservative orientation, leading to emphatic rejection of new ideas.

The "received edicts" of the Yi dynasty were not publicly promulgated or made widely available to the general public; they were simply conveyed to the lower offices. When a codification was completed, it was presented to the king. With his approval (*kanap*), the compilation was printed and distributed to the government agencies. Thus there was no date for the promulgation of codes; only the date of enforcement was set for the offices concerned.

Since the laws were conveyed only to the lower offices, the officials were the only persons knowledgeable of and responsible for the application of the laws, and the laws were applied to the common people who, in turn, were responsible not for knowing the laws but for obeying the officials. This practice seems to reflect the influence of Confucian paternalism. In the *Analects*, Confucius had said: "The people may be made to follow a path of action, but they may not be made to understand it."[21] This principle of nonpromulgation was strictly observed throughout the Yi dynasty. Political participation by the general public was prohibit-

---

[21] Legge, *The Chinese Classics*, I:211.

ed; the people were not allowed even to be informed about politics or law, but were only controlled and supervised by the government and penalized or restrained when they disobeyed. Such a system has no room for notions of freedom or rights for the common people.

Distinction of status was a major premise of Korean political and social organization. Confucian teachings, as found in the *Analects* and in Mencius' writings, make a distinction between the nobles (referred to as superior men, great men, officials or ministers) and commoners (*sangin*) who were held in low esteem and often called *ssangnom* (vulgar fellows). Mencius once said: "That whereby man differs from the lower animals is but small. The mass of people cast it away while superior men preserve it."[22] In such a society, Confucian morality and ritual conduct or manners (*ye*) constituted the rules to be followed by the *yangban* class. All social norms, including the codified laws, functioned to solidify and preserve the relative position of the rulers and the ruled. Moreover, the ancient *Li chi* had asserted: "Punishment is not applied to the gentleman and the code of manners (*ye*) is not applied to the common people." This meant that the *yangban* were immune from the enforcement of criminal law. The *yangban* class was subject to a "politics of virtue," regulated through rules of deportment, while the common people were subject to a politics of laws and punishments.

Laws and punishments were designed to reinforce the status distinction. For example, there was a saying that "when the punishments are severe, the mean [common people] will not dare to transgress against the noble; when laws are fierce, the hierarchical order will not be violated." While the common people looked upon laws with fear, they regarded the *yangban* officials who enforced the laws with even greater fear. Dallet points out the oppression of the common people by the *yangban*:

> When a *yangban* has no money, he orders his servants to arrest a merchant or a farmer who seems to be wealthy. If he is able to pay voluntarily, the *yangban* would release him. But if he would not bring the amount of money to the house of the nobleman, he would be imprisoned, beaten and not given food until he paid the amount of money asked.[23]

In the countryside, the *yangban* was especially feared. The expression "the *yangban* is coming!" was used to stop the crying of babies. The people were also afraid of the laws, the rules of deportment, and Confucian

[22] Ibid., II:325.

[23] Charles Dallet, *Traditional Korea*, Behavior Science Translations from Charles Dallet, *Histoire de l'Eglise de Corée: Introduction* (New Haven: Human Relations Area Files, 1954), p. 103.

morality; to them[24] all were complicated and formidable. As Montesquieu pointed out in *The Spirit of the Laws*, Chinese despotism was based on the principle of fear;[25] this may be applied equally to other East Asian societies.

For the upper class, then, law was understood as being supplementary to the practice of morals and deportment. If morals and *ye* were the primary social norms, law provided secondary norms, aimed at punishing those who broke the primary norms; penal law was a coercive apparatus which ensured that morals and *ye* were duly observed. If morals and *ye* were the ideal norms (*Zwecknorm*), legal norms were the means (*Mittelsnorm*) by which these moral norms were actualized and reinforced. Legal norms were subsumed under the category of moral norms. Chŏng To-jŏn asserted: "When a sage ruler makes a law, it is not designed for governing but only as a means to aid in governing." Several centuries later Yi Ik (1681–1763) also said that "law is based on the *ye*. Institutions are established in accordance with *ye*; social order and penalties exist [to handle] violations. This is what is meant by law. If laws are not based on *ye*, the word law becomes an empty term."[26] As indicated in these quotations, laws were understood to be no more than a means to an end.

The traditional perception of law did not recognize the importance of law, and this in turn gave rise to the idea that it could be disregarded or need not be applied strictly—at least not to the *yangban* who had direct access to the underlying system of moral norms, the protection of which was the sole purpose of the law. The law was perceived as applicable only to those who did not know the underlying moral norms, that is, the common people and "barbarians." The following statement from the *Ch'un Ch'iu* asserts that law was principally to be used in governing only the uncivilized, ignorant, or barbarian peoples: "It is morality whereby China is ruled; it is by punishment that the wild tribes around China are ruled by awe."[27]

Since laws were merely tools to govern the lower class people and the uncivilized barbarians around China, they were not deemed of importance by the *yangban* as objects of interest or worthy or study. In the words of the T'ang poet Su Shih who held the law in proud disdain, "Read ten thousand books but not the law." Reading books on law was not something which *yangban* gentlemen did. Officials responsible for legal matters

[24] Ibid., p. 104.

[25] Charles Louis de Secondat Montesquieu, *De l'Esprit des Lois*, ed. J. P. Mayer and A. P. Kerr (Paris: Gallimard, 1970), p. 156.

[26] Yi Ik, *Sŏngho Saesŏl* (Seoul: Minjok Munhwa Chujinhoe, 1978), VII:273.

[27] Legge, *The Chinese Classics*, V:196.

were selected on the basis of examination; not the Civil Service examination (*mungwa*), the literary examination which was monopolized by the *yangban* class, but one of several miscellaneous technical examinations. Only those who passed the literary examination could rise to the high-ranking posts of government; those who passed the legal examination were limited to the technical posts below the sixth degree of official rank. Thus the *yangban* class did not have to study law and indeed did not seek to do so. Chŏng Yag-yong (1762–1836), a leading scholar of the "practical learning" (*sirhak*) school, points out this phenomenon in his handbook for magistrates, *Mongmin simsŏ*:

> Today's gentlemen usually spend their time enjoying the poems of Hsiang Yu or P'ei Kung. When they become bored, they devote themselves to the high skills required to play flower cards and dominos.

Chŏng lamented the fact that legal matters, sometimes involving decisions of life or death, were manipulated by the lower-rank officials and even by courtesans to unjustly sentence the innocent.

This contempt of law and lack of interest in legal studies on the part of the governing class created a political environment in which laws could be ignored with impunity by the *yangban*. The many cases where peasants or merchants were confined and privately punished in *yangban* houses show that the *yangban* lived outside the law. The leading newspaper at the end of the Yi dynasty, the *Hwangsŏng Sinmun*, described the situation at that time:

> In the life of the poor common people there are too many things to be put up with. First, it is almost impossible to find magistrates who are pure and who help the people; most of them are corrupt and regard the people as their meat and fish. Through various means they make a business of extorting money. Once a person is arrested, a considerable sum of money is made, irrespective of his guilt or innocence. Once captured by the officials, suspects are beaten and restrained in irons without any investigation of evidence, and detained for months without being interrogated, only to be released when the magistrate has had his fill of yellow gold. Without money for bribes, even innocent people have no means to rectify the injustice; they suffer. How can the people withstand this kind of situation?[28]

Memorials to the Yi-dynasty kings frequently include phrases such as this one from the Shoo King: "The people are the root of a country; if

[28] *Hwangsŏng Sinmun*, 11 December 1900.

the root is solid, the country could be peaceful and stable."[29] Similar statements have occasionally been used to support the argument that the Yi dynasty embraced the concept of rule "for the benefit of the people." Although Confucian teachings include such phrases as "for the people" or "love the people," these are political ideas whose social premise was a feudal society and are quite different in meaning from the modern Western democratic principle of government "for the people," based on a concept of human equality and dignity.

Roman law assumed that people have different (and conflicting) interests in their social life, and law was therefore defined as rendering to each his due: *voluntas ius suum cuique*.[30] In this view, law defines the limits of the power of individuals to further their own interests. The extent to which these limits are observed determines the justice or injustice of the system. In other words, laws exist to realize justice. Modern Western legal systems, developed from the Roman tradition of law, function to realize this unique purpose of law—social justice.

In contrast, Oriental legal systems—including that of the Yi dynasty—were based on the premise that social life is to be regulated by moral norms, *ye* in the general sense. The purpose of laws was to punish those who violated the principles of social morality. Law was used as a means to achieve the ends defined by the moral code and had no autonomous function. The goal was to arrive at a society ruled not by law but by Confucian morals. The Confucian ideal society could be achieved by establishing harmony between the social norms and the law of nature upon which the human social order was said to be based. In other words, the ideal society was the "society of great peace," a society where harmonious relationships are maintained between the ruling and the ruled classes and in which the ruled are satisfied with the status quo. Confucius said:

> If the people be led by laws and uniformity sought to be given them by punishments, they will try to avoid the laws but have no sense of shame. If they be led by virtue, and uniformity sought to be given them by the rules of propriety, they will have a sense of shame and moreover will become good.[31]

Society, then, was government by men, a government which looked for leaders of wisdom and virtue. With rulers like Yao and Shun the rule of

---

[29] Legge, *The Chinese Classics*, III:158.

[30] *Corpus Juris Civilis*, Digestorum sec Pandectarum, I:10.

[31] Legge, *The Chinese Classics*, I:146.

virtue was possible, not not with rulers like Chieh or Chou. The rule of morality meant government by men not by laws, in contrast with the government of laws not men, which was the goal of Western law.[32]

The moral norms of Confucian society existed to prevent criminal acts; the laws (or punishments) were regarded as deterrents to crime. The realization of morality or the norms of *ye* would mean the disappearance of crimes and of the need for laws and punishments. Accordingly, traditional Confucian thought during the Yi dynasty understood an ideal society to be one of "empty prisons" and "government without punishment." It was customary for the official historians of the Yi dynasty to memorialize reports claiming that "the prisons are empty" and to record this in the Veritable Records.

Punishment was therefore justified to prevent further punishment,[33] and laws were applied only in the expectation that the use of law would one day end. The kings of the Yi dynasty held to this ideal, and every king issued edicts for the easing of penalties. Sŏngjong in particular cited these classical phrases explicitly in his admonition to the governors of the eight provinces,[34] and emphasized the value of human life while calling for the building of a society of "great peace" in which enforcement of laws would be unnecessary. Toward the end of the Yi dynasty, the poet Yi Tŏk-ham expressed his longing for such an ideal society, so free of legal disputes that the magistrate had no cases to judge:

> Birds play in the court yard;
> the magistrate's rule is pure, and he hears no disputes.
> More upright than any other in hearing disputes, still
> he knows: "no litigation is best."[35]

Dr. Bong Duck Chun serves as president of the Korean Legal Center in Seoul and is recognized as the dean of Korean legal studies having taught that subject for many years. He has published widely in Korea on legal subjects.

[32] "Massachusetts Bill of Rights," Art. 30, Henry Steele Commager, ed., *Documents of American History* (Englewood Cliffs, New Jersey: Prentice-Hall, 1973), p. 110.

[33] Legge, *The Chinese Classics*, III:58–59.

[34] *Chosŏn Wangjo Sillok*, IX:424.

[35] Myŏnggyun Sin, *Sijo Chŏnjip* [The Complete Works of Korean Verse], p. 174.

Social and Intellectual Aspects of Traditional Korean Law, 1392–1910

William Shaw

Since the publication of Hahm Pyong-choon's articulate survey of the Korean legal and political tradition,[1] it might seem that any study of Korean legal history must begin by contending with a strong presumption against the significance, not to say the existence, of its subject matter. Hahm's arguments, and those of other Korean scholars, may be summarized as follows: Traditional Korean political philosophy, in both its institutional and theoretical aspects, was based on "Confucian" precepts, and hence law and legal institutions were undervalued and despised. The primary mechanism for government at all levels was presumed to be the force of the moral example of those in authority. Moreover, the hierarchical structure of Korean society undermined the growth of law, as particularistic distinctions of social status and official position and the force of social convention precluded the possibility of predictability in judicial decision making.

---

[1] Hahm Pyong-choon, *The Korean Political Tradition and Law* (Seoul: Hollym, 1967). The "Korean view of law" as presented by Hahm bears a striking resemblance to the view of law found in Plato's *Republic*. More recently, Chŏn Pong-dŏk has summarized the deficiencies of traditional Korean law under five headings: (1) Korean law was merely the will and command of the sovereign; (2) Korean legislation was hampered by the principle that the older of two conflicting statutes took precedence; (3) Korean law was bureaucratic in character, laws being addressed to officials and not the populace at large; (4) laws existed exclusively for the benefit of the elite *yangban* class; (5) law was subordinated to considerations of morality in an arbitrary manner. Chŏn Pong-dŏk, "Chŏnt'ongjŏk sahoe wa pŏpsasang [Traditional Korean Society and Legal Thought]," *Pŏphak* [*Seoul Law Journal*], 19:1 (August, 1978), 52–66.

The presumption is significant for several reasons. If the entire notion of law was alien and illegitimate in traditional Korea, it would be misleading to use even the most general Western legal terminology in describing Korea, because the underlying basis of ideas would be so different that no common universe of discourse would exist.[2] A double smoke screen, made up of our own underlying legal preconceptions and the fact of the irrelevance of Korean "legal" phenomena—which would now be reduced to mere rhetoric—would obscure the "real" operant factors in Korean history. One's time would be better spent in determining what those primary factors were and in exploring them.

The nature of traditional Korean law also has important implications for the study of Korean economic history. Many historians have argued that the climate of legal thought in a premodern society is not irrelevant to the question of economic development. If legal rationality—including notions of regularity and predictability—was lacking or deficient in the Korean tradition, perhaps it would be well to reconsider the work of those Korean scholars who have been busily finding signs of an "early modern" economy in the "capital accumulation" of every peasant entrepreneur and wealthy peddler.[3]

Vindication of the thesis that law was intellectually and institutionally insignificant in traditional Korea would also provide an insight into Korea's lack of success in adapting to international political life in the late

---

[2] See Adda B. Bozeman, *The Future of Law in a Multicultural World* (Princeton, N.J.: Princeton University Press, 1971), chap. 1. Frederick Mote, writing of China's intellectual tradition, states that "law could scarcely be expected to achieve the significance it possessed in civilizations where it was based on a superrational and unchallengeable law of God . . ." and urges more scholarly attention to the as yet "ill-detected cosmological gulf [that] separates Western civilization, as well as other civilizations including Eastern ones, from Chinese civilization." *Intellectual Foundations of China* (New York: Knopf, 1971), pp. 26–28.

[3] For a sophisticated reinvestigation and elaboration of the Weber thesis on the association between religious, legal, and economic thought and activity, see David Little, *Religion, Order and Law: A Study in Pre-Revolutionary England* (New York: Harper & Row, 1969). An excellent series of bibliographical essays (on pp. 226–259) review the literature on this complex question. For a representative example of scholarship that asserts the "early modern" character of the late Yi dynasty economy, see Kang Man-gil, "Chosŏnhugi sangŏpchabon ŭi sŏngjang [The Growth of Commercial Capital in the Later Chosŏn (Yi) Period]," *Han'guksa yŏn'gu* [*Studies in Korean History*], 1 (1968–69), 79–107. Kang's article focuses on the capital accumulation of large-scale merchants and the "infiltration" of this accumulated capital into various areas of production. A survey of the work of Kang and others on this question has been done by Kim Yŏng-ho, "Chosŏn hugi e issŏsŏ ŭi tomae sisangŏp ui saeroun palchŏn [The Development of Wholesale Marketing in the Later Chosŏn (Yi) Period]," *Han'guksa yŏn'gu*, 2 (December, 1968), 25–52.

nineteenth century. To factors of economic backwardness, political incompetence, and military weakness might be added the factor of Confucian purity so great that no adjustment to the merely legalistic thought forms of encroaching imperialism could have been possible.[4] Apart from the overwhelming problems of a material nature, Korean statesmen could not even have understood the terms of dialogue or the structure of modern international economic or political relations. In every sphere, then, economic, political, and intellectual, Korea would serve as a model of a "traditional society," that is, a society by definition incapable of becoming part of the nineteenth-century world, given the short lead time available, without changes of a revolutionary nature in every area of thought and activity.

Finally, the nature of traditional Korean legal thought and institutions has an important bearing on the study of Korean legal development in the twentieth century. Undoubtedly, the more recent past—the period under Japanese colonial rule—has exerted a more potent influence on Korean legal development in the postwar era than has the more remote legacy of Yi-dynasty law. Yet residual influences from the precolonial period may also be discerned, particularly in family law, but in other areas as well. Some understanding of Yi-dynasty law is also important for the study of the impact of Japanese colonial legal institutions on Korean legal development, because it was against the traditional legacy that Japanese law and policy had to contend, just as postwar Korean society and government have had to come to terms with the colonial legacy.

The present study can do no more than outline some key areas that must be examined if the traditional "baseline" of modern Korean legal development is to be properly understood in its historical context. Since those writers who have most strongly suggested that traditional law was devoid of positive elements for the development of "modern" legal institutions and legal consciousness in Korea have stressed the role played by

[4] Korean and Western writers have long indicted Korean thought forms as partially or largely responsible for the diplomatic disasters of the nineteenth century. See Mary C. Wright, "The Adaptability of Ch'ing Diplomacy: The Case of Korea," *Journal of Asian Studies*, 17:3 (1958), 363–381; and Frederick M. Nelson, *Korea and the Old Orders in Eastern Asia* (Baton Rouge, La.: Louisiana State University Press, 1945). On the Korean side, see Yi Pyŏng-do, *Han'guksa taegwan* [*A Survey of Korean History*] (Seoul: Pŏmunsa, 1969), pp. 475–476, for a typical summary of the shortcomings of Korean neo-Confucianism. Sohn Pow-key, "The Opening of Korea: A Conflict of Traditions," *Transactions of the Korea Branch of the Royal Asiatic Society*, 36 (1960), adopts the "Confucian purity" approach. Hahm Pyong-choon's arguments in "Korea's Initial Encounter with the [*sic*] Western Law: 1866–1910 A.D.," *Korean Observer*, 1:2 (January, 1969), 80–93, are likewise based on the apparent premise that Korean thought forms, or "ideology" as he terms them, were inherently incompatible with those of the West and could only persist in hermitlike isolation or be obliterated under the guns and treaties of Japanese and Western imperialism.

Yi-dynasty thought and social structure, this study will discuss these two subjects.

The first two sections below examine the intellectual basis of traditional Korean law as manifested in general writings on political theory, judicial reasoning used in deciding specific cases, and the nature and development of Yi-dynasty law and legislation. The final two sections deal with aspects of the interrelation between law and society in the Yi period, with some attention paid to the topics of social inequality and legal aspects of local society and government.

LEGAL VALUES AND LEGAL THOUGHT IN TRADITIONAL KOREA

Law in Korean Political Theory

Until relatively recently, studies of the Chinese and Korean legal traditions have stressed the great gulf that presumably divided those traditions from the legal thought and institutions of early-modern and modern Europe. Where modern European legal systems were held to be secular, impersonal, and rational, Chinese law was said to remain subordinated to the individual moral insights of the judge and his desire to administer law by taking people and circumstances into account in a particularistic fashion.[5] Confucian thought made the matter worse, it was argued, by making the use of moral suasion the paramount tool of monarchical leadership and casting a pall of illegitimacy over the use of laws and punishments.[6] In Korea, as in China, it was said that judges looked to the "circumstances" of each case (*chŏng*, Chinese *ch'ing*) rather than to the statutory law (*pŏp*, Chinese *fa*).[7] Thus the Western concept implied by the phrase "rule of law" would have signified to Chinese or Korean thinkers simply a virtually immoral use of naked force in punishing the ineducable or perverted;[8] resort to law in this manner represented a failure of moral leadership on the part of the sovereign[9] and could never become a desirable political goal.[10]

---

[5] Max Weber, *The Religion of China: Confucianism and Taoism*, trans. Hans Gerth (Glencoe, Ill: The Free Press, 1951).

[6] Ch'ü T'ung-tsu, *Law and Society in Traditional China* (Paris and the Hague: Mouton, 1961); Arthur Waley, *Three Ways of Thought in Ancient China* (London: Macmillan, 1939); and Hahm, *Korean Political Tradition*.

[7] *The Treatise on Criminal Law from the Draft Official History of the Ch'ing Dynasty*, trans. Chang Wejen (unpublished manuscript, 1978), p. 90.

[8] Hahm, *Korean Political Tradition*, p. 45.

[9] Ibid., pp. 29–30.

[10] Ibid., p. 21.

We will discuss this topic in the context of two questions: (1) did Yi-dynasty thinkers regard law as a legitimate part of government, and what did they feel should be the role of law? and (2) what can be learned about Korean legal values from the analysis of case decisions?

Law and Confucianism—Recent studies of the Chinese intellectual and legal traditions have suggested that the early twentieth-century Western portrait of Chinese law and legal thought is overdrawn, even for the classical period of Confucian thought, sixth to third centuries B.C.[11] Moreover, it must be remembered that the form of Confucian thought which eventually prevailed in Yi-dynasty Korea was not that of the ancient Chou period but rather Confucianism as developed in the writings of the neo-Confucian thinkers of the Southern Sung dynasty (A.D. 1127–1279). For example, the commentaries of Chu Hsi (1130–1200) on the works of the classical period make it clear that he did not reject penal law in favor of the power of moral example, but that he regarded the two as complementary aspects of an integrated whole; neither aspect could be unilaterally discarded.[12]

These ideas were introduced in Korea in their most developed form in the writings of Chŏng To-jŏn (d. 1398), particularly in his *Chosŏn kyŏnggukchŏn* [*Law for the Government of Korea*], a treatise on government presented to the Yi-dynasty founder Yi Sŏng-gye.[13] Like Chu Hsi, Chŏng viewed punitive or disciplinary law as an indispensable tool of government. Legal sanctions were seen as a vital aspect of all branches of administration. Tax and revenue administration, for example, could not be divorced from penal sanctions needed to punish evasion, or official malfeasance. State rituals and religious practices likewise required that incorrect performance be punished.[14] "Punishments are required for ceremonies to realize themselves."[15]

[11] Derk Bodde and Clarence Morris, *Law in Imperial China* (Cambridge, Mass.: Harvard University Press, 1967); Chen Fu-mei Chang, "Private Code Commentaries in the Development of Ch'ing Law (1644–1911)," unpublished Ph.D. dissertation (Harvard University, 1970); Paul Chen, "Chih-yuan hsin-ko; the Yuan Code of 1291 as Reconstructed and a Survey of Yuan Legal Institutions," unpublished Ph.D. dissertation (Harvard University, 1973); and Hsu Dau-lin, "Crime and Cosmic Order," *Harvard Journal of Asiatic Studies*, 30 (1970), 111–125. A recent work that takes the older view is Roberto M. Unger's *Law in Modern Society* (New York: Free Press, 1976), pp. 86–110.

[12] *Sasŏ* (*The Four Books*), facsimile of an eighteenth-century Korean edition of the Four Books with Chu Hsi commentaries (Seoul, 1972), p. 78.

[13] See Chŏng To-jŏn, *Sambongjip* [*Collected Writings of Sambong* (*Chŏng To-jŏn*)] (Seoul: Kuksa p'yŏnch'an wiwŏnhoe [National History Compilation Committee], 1961).

[14] Ibid., p. 247.

[15] Ibid., p. 241.

Even the ruler's responsibility to transform his officials and his subjects through the force of moral example, a common theme in Chinese and Korean Confucian thought, did not obviate the need for legal mechanisms. Thus, in commenting on Ming Code provisions dealing with forgery and bribery, Chŏng wrote: "If the sovereign clarifies the distinction between profit and moral probity and thereby encourages a sense of shame, both problems [of forgery and bribery] can eventually be eradicated. But the penal statutes may nonetheless not be abandoned."[16]

Thought of the later Yi dynasty also emphasized the use of law in government, a circumstance reflected in several reprintings of Chŏng To-jŏn's work.[17] The *sirhak* or "practical learning" encyclopedist Yi Ik (1681–1763), for example, explicitly declared his affinity with the legal thought of Han Fei tzu, though he did not go so far as the famous legalist thinker in downgrading the role that moral example and instruction might play in government.[18]

Yi Ik's student and editor, An Chŏng-bok (1712–1791), felt that moral instruction was generally superior to punishment, but he also argued that magistrates had a duty to keep the populace informed about provisions of the criminal law,[19] and he urged strict punishment of heterodox religious practices at the village level.[20] Like Chŏng To-jŏn, An stressed the holistic nature of ethical and institutional-legal considerations in governnent: "Institutions and laws and ethical transformation are not, at heart, two separate entities. Rather, ethical transformation is the 'end' of good government, and institutions and law the 'means.'"[21]

In this respect, although by the later Yi period many of the specific issues and problems facing Korean society and government had changed, there is little to distinguish Korean legal values of the seventeenth and eighteenth centuries from those expressed by Chŏng To-jŏn as part of his blueprint for the Yi dynasty in the late fourteenth century. Some commentators might stress the institutional, others the moral components of government reform, in accordance with what they perceived as the need of the moment, without departing from the underlying neo-Confucian vi-

---

[16] Ibid., p. 245.

[17] For the publication history of the *Sambongjip*, see page 6 of Sin Sŏk-ho's introduction to the edition cited in note 13, above.

[18] Yi Ik, *Sŏngho saesŏl yusŏn* [*Digest of the Collectanea of Sŏngho* (Yi Ik)], ed. An Chŏng-bok (Seoul: Chōsen kankōkai [Society for the Publication of Korean Books], 1915), I, 393.

[19] An Chŏng-bok, *Imgwan chŏng'yo* [*Essentials for Government*] (Seoul: Ŭryu munhwasa, 1974), p. 322.

[20] Ibid., p. 319.

[21] Ibid., pp. 306–307.

sion of government as requiring both good men and effective laws and institutions.[22] In short, the use of penal law was not merely tolerated, *faute de mieux*, much less thought of as an indication of moral failure on the part of the ruler,[23] but was assumed to be an indispensable tool of government.

Korean Legal Thought in Action

What was Korean legal thinking like in the practice of legal administration? The answer may be found by examining criminal case records and the reasoning used to adjudicate such cases. Fairly brief abstracts of criminal cases exist in several sources.[24] These case briefs rarely provide more than the name of the criminal and the crime committed, together with a citation of the statute applied and the final sentence. For more insight into Korean legal thought, we must turn to the records generated by the *simni* review process. This process was established to provide special high-level reviews of problematic cases involving the death penalty. About one thousand of these case records are contained in a late eighteenth-century compilation, the *Simnirok*.[25] The following analysis is largely based on translation and study of a representative sample of one hundred of these cases. The reasoning of the king and high officials in discussing and settling these cases reveals important aspects of Korean legal thought and practice, aspects that cannot be understood on the basis of general philosophical writings alone.

One example of such reasoning is what the records tell us of how punishments were justified in Korea. Some students of the Korean legal tradition have cited the ancient Chinese aphorism that "through punishment there may come to be no more punishments,"[26] with its implication that law is a temporary expedient; in other words, as civilization advances, crime and punishment will fade away. This aphorism (and the

[22] See Yu Su-wŏn, *Usŏ* [*Writings of an Outsider*], facsimile edition (Seoul: Sŏul taehakkyo kojŏn kanhaenghoe [Seoul National University Classics Publication Society], 1971), p. 39c, where the author argues that the Sung, T'ang, Han, and *Chou li* precedents be applied in instituting legal examinations for government officials.

[23] Hahm, *Korean Political Tradition*, pp. 29–30.

[24] See Pak Il-wŏn, ed., *Ch'ugwanji* [*Treatise on the Board of Punishments*] (Keijō [Seoul]: Chōsen sōtokufu chūsūin [Chōsen Government-General Secretariat], 1939); and *Yullye yoram* [*Conspectus of Laws and Precedents*] (1837?), in *Sugyo chŏngnye—Yullye yoram* [*Received Edicts Enacted as Precedents—Conspectus of Laws and Precedents*] (Seoul: Pŏpchech'ŏ [Office of Legislation], 1970).

[25] *Simnirok* [*Records of Simni Review Hearings*], 2 vols. (Seoul: Pŏpchech'ŏ, 1968).

[26] James Legge, trans., *The Chinese Classics*, 5 vols. (Hong Kong: Hong Kong University Press, 1960), III, 541–542. The quotation is from the *Shu ching* [*Book of History*].

underlying sentiment), however, appears only rarely in the case records. More frequent are phrases such as "killing the criminal so others can live" (*saengdo sarin*), which have no classical pedigree but which reflect a utilitarian conception that protection of society is a valid function of criminal law.[27]

Requital for a life—Perhaps an even more important motive for prosecution of a murderer, if the case records are any indication, was the principle of "requital for a life" (*sangmyŏng*). Students of traditional Chinese law have suggested that the corresponding Chinese term, *ti-ming*, implied a rather simple substitution. The death of the victim had upset the cosmic balance, as it were, and it became the government's task to redress the balance. Such redress is held to have been almost mechanistic; restoration of the balance and of cosmic harmony is supposed to have outweighed mere evidentiary considerations, and almost any life would do.[28] This view has been subjected to challenge from the Chinese perspective, and the Korean materials also suggest that the concept of requital, though important, must be understood differently.[29]

In the traditional Korean view (and, I would suggest, in the traditional Chinese view as well), both sociological and religious considerations underlay the concept of requital. Chinese and Korean writings indicate that the desire of a murder victim's kin for vengeance was legitimate and was to be assuaged, provided the principal offender could be determined. A religious element was involved because the victim's personality was deemed to continue after death and to share in the desire for requital as a "grieved ghost," or *wŏngwi* in modern parlance. If the government failed to prosecute and punish the culprit, the grievance of the deceased would ascend to heaven, and heaven would visit disturbances of nature—unseasonable weather, drought, or worse—upon the state. It was mispunishment that upset the cosmic balance, not the crime.

The notion of requital for a life is especially important for its contributions to Korean attitudes toward procedure and evidence, because requital was a two-edged concept. To be effective, requital had to be *true* requital: only the actual murderer would suffice, and in Sino-Korean theory he had to be fully culpable. (A less than fully culpable suspect would have his own grievance if wrongfully executed.) Wrongful punishment was an act of misgovernment with cosmic implications.

Many grounds for reduced individual culpability existed in Chinese law—for example, participation of several individuals in a slaying, the

[27] See *Simnirok*, case of An Ch'il-gŭm, I, 30, 58–59; and case of Kim Ok-chae, I, 77–78, 136–137, 372.

[28] Bodde and Morris, *Law in Imperial China*, p. 331.

[29] Hsu Dau-lin, "Crime and Cosmic Order," p. 124.

weakened or sickly prior condition of the victim, or insufficient evidence against a single suspect—and so the review process in murder cases became a careful search to see whether such grounds for clemency existed. The result was an impressive concern for "careful investigation of cases" (*simsin, simgŭk*), which amounted in practice to close scrutiny of procedural and evidentiary considerations. This may be thought of as a functional equivalent to "due process," although with a different historical and philosophical basis from that underlying the notion of due process in the West.

"Law" and "circumstances"—The case records also clarify the Korean usage of a major conceptual distinction, that between "law" (*pŏp*) and "circumstances" (*chŏng*). These terms or their equivalents occur frequently in the case records as the king discussed the cases with his officials. In looking at this from a modern perspective, it has often seemed that the term "circumstances" was used to disguise various particularistic or extralegal grounds for judgment. Thus the king sometimes made statements to the effect that "the law requires the death penalty in this case, but the circumstances provide grounds for clemency." This would seem to have been a highly subjective form of reasoning.

Examination of the use of these terms suggests several points. The first is that there were indeed some cases in which the term "circumstances" was used to introduce extralegal considerations and to give a lighter sentence than the law or material evidence would seem to dictate. Such cases generally concerned a defendant of higher social status than the victim, although higher social status did not ensure favorable treatment in every case. A second point is that in the majority of cases where "law" and "circumstances" were cited, the two were held to be in agreement; the king argued that both law and circumstances dictated the sentence he was awarding. In such instances statutory and legal considerations evidently dominated the decision, and "circumstances" were adduced in a formulaic manner to provide verbal undergirding. In the third kind of situation, the term "circumstances" was used to refer to the question of intent in a murder case. Since the law distinguished between intentional and unintentional homicide, intent had to be considered. Yet the code did not provide exhaustive guidelines for determining intent, and a subjective element unavoidably entered into the resolution of the case. Questions like this, introducing the troublesome concept of *mens rea*, are difficult to resolve in any legal system, because determining the state of mind of a defendant at the time of a crime cannot be reduced to clear-cut rational criteria, and judgment must always involve the insights and common sense of the judge.[30] In summary, the murder cases of the *Sim-*

[30]See Helen Silving, *Criminal Justice*, 2 vols. (Rio Piedras, Puerto Rico: Hein,

nirok do not show that the concept of "circumstances" was generally used to subjectively manipulate judgments, although some instances of manipulation can be found.

Conclusion

Korean writings on political theory and the specific reasoning used in resolving criminal cases suggest a number of conclusions concerning the role of law in Korean society and Korean legal concepts.

First, law, including criminal law, was not devalued but was highly regarded. This may be seen not only in the comments of political thinkers like Chŏng To-jŏn and An Chŏng-bok, for whom law was as indispensable as morality in good government, but also, as will be noted in the following section, in the resources and careful attention devoted to codification during the dynasty.

Second, there was a manifest concern in case records like those of the *Simnirok* for factual accuracy, substantive legal precision, and procedural niceties. In murder cases, at least, the techniques of forensic medicine were painstakingly applied to ascertain the probable cause of death.[31] Since numerous instances can be found where local officials were disciplined for infractions in the conduct of inquests or other aspects of the investigative process, it may be supposed that the quality of official legal expertise was higher among central government legal officials than among county-level officials in the provinces. Yet such discipline also suggests that at least some formal checks existed to curb technical incompetence or abuses of position at the local level.

The cases suggest that the legal reasoning of the king and high legal officials was generally rational in a formal legal sense. Considerations of personal moral insight, social status distinctions, or policy considerations did at times intrude into the process of judgment, but such intrusions seem to have been exceptional.

The concept of "requital for a life" and the concomitant concern for "careful investigation of cases" lest a less than fully culpable person be executed resulted in the state assuming a heavy burden of proof against defendants in murder cases. Cases in which the death penalty was imposed for murder were rare, accounting for only about 2 percent of all *simni* review cases in the late eighteenth century.

Finally, the discussions between the king and his ministers in deliberating problematic cases provide an intriguing insight into the nature of the Korean monarchy. Although the king, acting as judge in such cases,

1971), II, 623–757. Silving here discusses comparative principles and cases related solely to the distinction between intent and negligence.

[31] *Chŭngsu muwŏllok* [*Amplified and Corrected Coroner's Guide for the Elimination of Grievances*] (Seoul: Pŏpchech'ŏ, 1975).

had the final word, he did not behave arbitrarily either toward the law or toward his advisory officials. The king was at pains to justify and argue out his position. This suggests that the Korean king was seen (and saw himself) as bound by the law and that he functioned, in this context at least, as "king in council" rather than as absolute monarch.[32]

SOURCES OF LAW AND THE LEGISLATIVE PROCESS IN YI DYNASTY KOREA, 1392–1910

The Role of Chinese Law

No understanding of the Yi-dynasty legal tradition is possible without coming to grips with the role of Chinese law and legal concepts in Korea during the Yi period. The penal code of the Ming dynasty, the *Ta-Ming lü*, though modified in some particulars by the effect of subsequent Korean legislation, was the basis for ciminal law in Korea from the time of its reception in the fifteenth century.[33] Some provisions, notably those pertaining to flogging as a penalty for Korean subjects, were retained in the code revisions of 1907–1908, which took place under Japanese auspices after the Japanese assumption of protectorate control over Korea.[34]

Chinese law, particularly that of the T'ang and Sung periods, was known in Korea before the Yi dynasty.[35] During the final decades of the preceding Koryŏ dynasty (918–1392), there had even been a short-lived attempt to make use of Yüan legislation.[36] Partly due to the pro-Ming diplomacy of the new regime of Yi Sŏng-gye, however, and partly due

[32]The ideological and institutional background of the relatively weak position of Yi dynasty sovereigns vis-à-vis the bureaucracy is detailed by Sohn Pow-key in "Social History of the Early Yi Dynasty," unpublished Ph.D. dissertation (University of California, Berkeley, 1963), chaps. 1 and 2. Political aspects of this situation are treated by Edward Willett Wagner in *The Literati Purges: Political Conflict in Early Yi Korea* (Cambridge, Mass.: 1974). For a summary statement on the Korean monarchy for the entire Yi period, see James B. Palais, "Political Leadership in the Yi Dynasty," in *Political Leadership in Korea*, by Suh Dae-sook and Lee Chae-jin (Seattle: University of Washington Press, 1976), pp. 4–15.

[33]*Kyŏngguk taejŏn* [*Great Code for Administering the Country*] (Keijō: Chōsen sōtokufu chūsūin, 1934), p. 469.

[34]For a discussion of the *Hyŏngpŏp taejŏn* [*Great Criminal Code*] of 1905 and subsequent reforms of 1907 and 1908, see John Sloboda, "Legal Change in Korea, 1876–1910: The Victory of Tradition," unpublished master's thesis (Harvard University, 1970), pp. 42–45, 54–56.

[35]Substantial similarities between T'ang and Koryŏ statutes are traced by Asami Rintarō in *Chōsen hōseishikō* [*Draft Legal History of Korea*] (Tokyo: Ganshō shoten, 1922), pp. 195–212.

[36]*Koryŏsa* [*History of Koryŏ*], *kwŏn* 84.30a.

to the greater clarity and level of organization of the Ming Code, it was the latter that was finally adopted in Korea. "Intelligibility of the law must be a primary concern of the ruler," argued a 1388 proponent of the Ming Code.[37]

This law appealed to the Yi-dynasty founder and his advisors because of its clarity and for legal, institutional, and conceptual reasons. These included a desire to establish clear jurisdictional lines between confused and competing judicial agencies, concern for careful review of death-penalty cases, and a determination that officials trying cases must adhere to code provisions and not introduce extraneous considerations into their judgments. Discussions in the late Koryŏ and early Yi periods of these and related questions reveal not only the shortcomings of the Koryŏ legal system but also the general familiarity of Korean thinkers and administrators with these fundamental values of the Chinese legal tradition.[38]

In sum, an important characteristic of Ming law for the bureaucrats and statesmen of the early Yi period was its rationality. The Ming Code was seen as valuable in the task of imposing order on the administration of justice and in the establishment of systematic disciplinary reform.[39] As a system of criminal law, the Ming Code was a coherent and self-consistent body of statutes that attempted to cover all possible circumstances, thereby reducing the risk of unwarranted judicial discretion.[40] Officials were expected to use code provisions and not their subjective moral or other insights in settling cases,[41] and penalties were provided for failure to accurately and fully cite the statute being applied.[42]

The Ming Code not only provided a basic foundation for criminal law during the Yi period, but also served as the basic foundation for a comprehensive social reform along neo-Confucian lines. This was accomplished by the increased criminalization of offenses among family

[37] Ibid., *kwŏn* 84.33b–36a.

[38] On the importance of the review of death penalty cases, see a memorial of A.D. 1018: *Koryŏsa chŏryo* [*Brief History of Koryŏ*], *kwŏn* 3.32b–33a. Following the text of the law in judicial decisions was the subject of a royal order of 1374: *Koryŏsa, kwŏn* 85.33b.

[39] *T'aejo sillok* [*Veritable Records of the Reign of King T'aejo*], *kwon* 1.44–45a, in *Chosŏn wangjo sillok* [*Veritable Records of the Chosŏn Dynasty*], 48 vols., index vol. (Seoul: Kuksa p'yŏnch'an wiwŏnhoe, 1968–1970), I, 22–23.

[40] *Koryŏsa, kwŏn* 84.33b–36a.

[41] Ibid.

[42] *Taemyŏngnyul chikhae* [*Directly Interpreted Ming Code*] (Seoul: Kyŏngin munhwasa, 1974), pp. 597–600, 601.

members, for example, as well as in other ways.[43] The Ming Code was in this respect the most thoroughly "Confucian" avatar of Chinese legal development.

Korean Legislation

Of course, Ming law was not the only law in effect in Korea, even during the early decades of the Yi period. A native administrative and penal code, the *Kyŏngje yukchŏn* (Six-Division Code for Administration), was promulgated as early as 1397.[44] Each of the six divisions of this code corresponded to one of the principal administrative boards of the central government, which generally was organized along Chinese lines as in the preceding Koryŏ period. Three revisions of this code were produced between 1413 and 1433. These became in turn the basis for the central legislative accomplishment of the early Yi dynasty, the *Kyŏngguk taejŏn* (Great Code for Administering the Country). This code stated explicitly that the Ming Code would be the basic criminal law of the dynasty, even while adding to Ming criminal law in important ways. Major supplements to the *Kyŏngguk taejŏn* appeared in 1746, 1785, and 1865. There is every indication that such legislative activity received a high priority in terms of personnel and other resources. Many scholars active in helping to draft the *Kyŏngguk taejŏn* were among the foremost literary and academic minds in the government, equally adept and accomplished in such diverse fields as Chinese phonology, history, and classics.[45] As important as Chinese law was in the Yi dynasty, then, it would be misleading to slight the significance of domestic codification and other forms of lawmaking.

What was the content of this Korean legislation? Essentially, Korean law developed to regulate positive programs of administration, including tax and population policies, ritual matters, and military organization, for which contemporary Chinese law offered little that could be applied to specifically Korean conditions. Thus, although the fifteenth-century *Kyŏngguk taejŏn* code stated that the Ming criminal code was to be used,[46] the penal statutes of the Korean compilation went on through more than twenty sections of law that amplified or differed from Ming law. Later, as Chinese and Korean case law continued to develop, supplementary cod-

---

[43] Kim Tu-hŏn, *Han'guk kajok chedo yŏn'gu* [*A Study of the Korean Family System*] *(Seoul:* Sŏul taehakkyo ch'ulp'anbu, 1969), pp. 163–167.

[44] Sŏ Il-gyo, *Chosŏn wangjo hyŏngsa chedo ŭi yŏn'gu* [*A Study of the Administration of Criminal Justice During the Chosŏn Dynasty*] (Seoul: Han'guk pŏmnyŏng p'yŏnch'anhoe [Korean Statutes Compilation Society], 1968), p. 33.

[45] See my "Traditional Korean Law and Its Relation to China," in *China's Legal Tradition*, ed. Jerome A. Cohen, et al. (Princeton, N.J.: Princeton University Press, 1980).

[46] *Kyŏngguk taejŏn*, p. 469.

ifications appeared in both countries, accentuating procedural and substantive divergences between the two.[47] Reflections of such divergences are not difficult to trace even in the first century of Yi rule. Korean slave-ownership customs and inheritance rules did not correspond to Chinese practice. Korea's conceptions of social-status distinctions were more ramified than those of China and found expression in sumptuary regulations and in criminal procedure. In some instances, actions not mentioned in the Ming Code were criminalized or penalties for specific offenses under Ming law were raised or lowered.

Despite the existence and growth of such distinctions, however, Korean criminal law never departed significantly from the fundamental theoretical categories of Chinese criminal law. A hypothetical visiting Chinese jurist might have been puzzled by the details of Korean penal statutes, but he would have found little theoretical novelty in Korean legislation or judicial reasoning. Many Korean code provisions remained keyed to the Ming Code, either explicitly or by analogy.[48] As in China, the categories of Ming law remained fundamental for generations of subsequent jurists (and officials).

Law and the Sovereign

The fiction was preserved throughout the Yi period that new laws were the result of spontaneous royal initiative, but in fact the position of Korean kings was institutionally weak. It would be more accurate to say that usually a Korean king presided over the deliberations of high ministers as *primus inter pares*. The position of the Korean king was reflected in the broad powers of royal lecturers, secretaries, and high officials to comment critically on state affairs and royal decisions, and the stress of the censorate organs on remonstrance rather than surveillance.[49] In principle, at least, all new laws (and most personnel appointments) were supposed to undergo "ratification" (*sŏgyŏng*) by the censorate and "certification" (*ŭich'ŏp*) by the Board of Rites.[50] How little the king participated in the creation of new law in the initial years of the dynasty may be seen in the recommendation of the State Council in 1404 that lower agencies of the government

[47] This process is discussed by Derk Bodde and Clarence Morris in *Law in Imperial China*, pp. 55–68. Code revisions were much more frequent in eighteenth- and nineteenth-century China than in Korea during the same period.

[48] In 1406, for example, the censorate proposed that the practice of submitting petitions directly before the royal carriage (*kajŏn chikchŏng*) be suspended and that violations should henceforth be punished according to the Ming Code statute on violation of royal edicts. *T'aejong sillok, kwŏn* 12.37b. This example could be multiplied.

[49] Sohn Pow-key, "Social History of the Early Yi Dynasty."

[50] *Kyŏngguk taejŏn*, p. 284.

"henceforward" submit new legislation to the State Council for discussion and that only after the king had made the final decision should new laws be put into effect![51]

The Lawmaking Process

The lawmaking process in the Yi period was essentially similar to that of Ming and Ch'ing China. Piecemeal incrementation of the existing body of law was more common than systematic legislation. The *Kyŏngje yukchŏn* of 1397, for example, had been made up of royal edicts from 1388 to the date of promulgation. Edicts could originate at the spontaneous initiative of the king, but more often they represented the king's response to a legal case or administrative proposal brought to his attention by a government agency or official. In the early part of the dynasty, special terms distinguished the two forms of lawmaking: but during the reign of Sejong (r. 1418–1450), the distinction was obliterated and a single term, *sugyo* (received edict), came to denominate both types, preserving the fiction that these were commands of the sovereign rather than his responses to the initiatives of others in the government.[52]

Such edicts were kept on file in the appropriate administrative agency of the government and were treated as binding precedents. Periodically such edicts were edited and published for the benefit of other central-government agencies and provincial and county-level officials. When such editing made a serious effort to eliminate deadwood and to resolve inconsistent or ambiguous edicts, the resulting compilation was termed a "code" (*chŏn*), with the implication that the laws therein would stand indefinitely, or at least until the compilation of the next code.[53] Less thoroughgoing efforts, amounting in practice to little more than the col-

[51] Cited by Chŏn Pong-dŏk in "Chŏnt'ong sahoe wa pŏpsasang," *Pŏphak*, 19:1 (January, 1978), 60.

[52] Ibid., pp. 60–61.

[53] Abrogation is, of course, an important characteristic of statutory law in the modern sense. See C. K. Allen, *Law in the Making* (London: Oxford University Press, 1958), pp. 409–410. Korean legal historians continue to be impressed with the concept sometimes expressed during the Yi period that law was unchangeable because it originated in the will of the "royal forebears." Thus, Chŏn Pong-dok "Chŏnt'ong sajoe wa pŏpsasang," p. 62, suggests that new law could only be effective to the extent that it did not contradict prior law. My own impression is somewhat different. The concept of the "law of the royal ancestors" was sometimes invoked during a policy discussion by high officials to attempt to limit the discretionary power of the king and subordinate the monarch to law. Sometimes this argument appears to have been effective. On the other hand, "codes" (*chŏn/jŏn*) clearly abrogated and revised earlier law, while paying lip service to the idea of continuity. This is a topic that requires further study. It was an established principle of Chinese law, of course, that newly promulgated statutes took precedence. See *Taemyŏngnul chikhae*, p. 104.

lection and reprinting of edicts on file, were termed "supplements" (*nok*). This process of compiling a code or supplement occurred seven times in the fifteenth century and somewhat less frequently thereafter.

YI DYNASTY CODES AND LEGISLATIVE COMPENDIA

"Codes" (*chŏn/jŏn*)	Edict Collections (*sugyo/nok*)
1397	
1413	
1426	
1433	
1470	
1474	
1485	
	1492
	1543
	1698
	1743
1746	
1785	
	1837
1865	

Rationality in Legislation

It was recognized in the later Yi period that piecemeal lawmaking in the manner described presented problems for regularity in law enforcement and rational administration. Edicts resolving difficult cases often clarified critical questions and made future judgments easier. This was entirely suitable as a means of filling in logical gaps in the Ming Code or in adjusting that law to the needs of Korean society while at the same time upholding the principle of legality and the broad principles embodied in the codified law. But the accumulation of edicts during a period of several reigns often produced a dense collection of overlapping or conflicting provisions–"ox hairs," in the words of one eighteenth-century critic. Unscrupulous officials or underlings, like common lawyers presented with two lines of precedent, liked to selectively "pull hairs" from this "great ox of the law" in order to raise or lower punishments in accordance with what the market could bear.[54] Even compilers of the periodic code supplements were reluctant to decide between two conflicting edicts and usually left

[54] Chŏng Sang-gi (1678–1752), *Nongp'o mundap* [*Conversations Between Farmer and Gardener*] (Seoul: Ŭryu munhwasa, 1974), p. 218.

both in.[55] Other edicts simply disappeared from the files over the years.[56] By the seventeenth and eighteenth centuries, the problems of merely keeping track of the total corpus of legislation, much less reconciling inconsistencies, were becoming nearly insurmountable.

Late Yi-dynasty governments used various methods to reduce the adverse impact of the traditional ad hoc approach to lawmaking. One important technique was to assign a particular administrative agency of the government the task of producing a legislative package containing interrelated provisions dealing with a given problem in some detail. This technique was not unknown in the early Yi period, but seems to have come into extensive use during the reign of King Sukchong (r. 1674–1720) and thereafter. These systematically drafted laws, or *samok*, were included together with ad hoc "received edicts" in edict collections and codes from this time onward.[57] This development represents a significant increase in the role of specialized legal-administrative expertise in the drafting of legislation and an important rationalizing influence on Korean law.

In criminal law, in the eighteenth century, two major contributions were made toward procedural standardization in *samok* dealing with inquest investigations[58] and the interrogation of criminal suspects.[59] Criminal-case records also show an increasing concern with the format of provincial case reports and the quality of local-government legal expertise.[60]

Our table of Yi-dynasty codes and other legislative compendia does not show the remarkable quantity and quality of publication of legal reference works that took place during the eighteenth century. The *Chŏllok t'onggo* (Conspectus of Code and Precedents) of 1706, for example, was a trial effort to simplify the task of legal officials and reduce the possibility for error by publishing under one set of covers the fifteenth-century *Kyŏngguk taejŏn* code and all subsequent legislation to date.[61] The *Soktaejŏn* (Supplementary Great Code) of 1746 further simplified legal

---

[55] *Sugyo chimnok* [*Promulgation of Received Edicts*], in *Jukyō shūyō* [*Collected Essential Edicts*] (Keijō: Chōsen sōtokufu chūsūin, 1943), p. 108.

[56] Ibid.

[57] For example, see a special law on ginseng trade promulgated in 1686 and included in the *Sugyo chimnok* of 1968. *Sugyo chimnok*, in *Jukyō shūyō*, pp. 219–220.

[58] *Chŏngjo sillok, kwŏn* 17.34b–35a.

[59] Ibid., *kwŏn* 5.5a–6a.

[60] *Sugyo chŏngnye*, pp. 38–39, 49–50.

[61] *Chŏllok t'onggo* [*Conspectus of Code and Precedents*] (Seoul: Pŏpchech'ŏ, 1969).

research by indicating the legislative origin of many of its provisions.[62] Other official publications of the late eighteenth century conveniently juxtaposed Ming Code provisions with Korean legislation[63] or provided convenient listings of Korean criminal laws filed according to the penalty inflicted.[64] The first collections of criminal-case records and decisions were also published at that time.[65]

THE INTERACTION OF LAW AND SOCIETY IN TRADITIONAL KOREA

Inequality

Considerations of social status played an important role in the structure and operation of the traditional Korean legal order. It has been suggested that a chief purpose of the codes was to rigidify class lines and protect the prerogatives of the upper classes against encroachment.[66] It is certainly not difficult to find some support for this view in the Korean codes themselves, though, as will be seen, some qualifications are necessary. In the criminal statutes of the *Kyŏngguk taejŏn* (1485), procedural and substantive provisions alike included extensive references to relative-status relationships. Prohibitions sometimes named groups of people exempt or otherwise deferred from the proscription.[67] In some situations, officials were required by law to report the status of those involved in a case in order to receive royal permission before arrest and detention or other procedures could be carried out.[68]

---

[62] *Soktaejŏn* [*Supplementary Great Code*] (Keijō: Chōsen sōtokufu chūsūin, 1935), p. 397; these are laws eliminating harsh penalties.

[63] *Chŏnyul t'ongbo* [*Conspectus of Chinese and Korean Codes*], 2 vols. (Seoul: Pŏpchech'ŏ, 1971).

[64] *(Chŭngbo) Munhŏn pigo* [*Supplemented Encyclopedia*], photolithograph of 1907 edition, 3 vols. (Seoul: Kojŏn Kanhaenghoe, 1957), vol. 3, *kwŏn* 136–139.

[65] *Simnirok*, 2 vols. (Seoul: Pŏpchech'ŏ, 1968); and *Ch'ugwanji* (Keijō: Chōsen sōtokufu chūsūin, 1939).

[66] Sŏ Il-gyo, *Chosŏn wangjo hyŏngsa chedo ŭi yŏn'gu*, p. 4; and Kim Yŏng-mo, *Chosŏn chibaech'ŭng yŏn'gu* [*A Study of the Ruling Class of Chosŏn*] (Seoul: Ilchogak, 1977), p. 18. The latter study contains (on pp. 16–17) the most recent and thorough treatment of legal aspects of Yi dynasty social structure. See also Yi Sŏng-mu, "Sibosegi yangbannon [On Fifteenth-Century *Yangban*]," *Ch'angjak kwa p'ip'yŏng*, 8:2 (Summer, 1973), 484–515 (especially p. 484).

[67] Kim Yŏng-mo, *Chosŏn chibaech'ŭng yŏn'gu*, p. 18, lists the following additional areas where differential provisions existed: taking examinations, appointment to office, exemption from labor service duties, rites and ceremonies, kinship lines, and clothing.

[68] *Kyŏngguk taejŏn*, p. 470: "In cases where the punishment is heavy bambooing or

Before proceeding further with the relationship of law and society in traditional Korea, I will briefly review some of the social categories that were differentiated in the Yi dynasty codes.[69] *Yangban* were members of hereditary houses entitled by station of birth to take the national literary examinations and serve in the higher civil service. Their economic position generally derived from ownership of land and slaves, which in turn often hinged on participation in national political life. The influence of *yangban* at the village level could stem from national political and familial ties, from local economic holdings, or, in the absence of these, from their position as educated and thus morally superior men.[70] *Sajok* ("noble families") and *sadaebu* ("official class") were the terms commonly used in the codes for *yangban*, respectively stressing lineage and political participatory aspects of their social identity. As the somewhat loose interrelation between ascriptive position and exercise of administrative-political authority suggests, there was a limited degree of mobility within *yangban* status and some degree of mobility out of it to lower levels. In the latter part of the Yi period, it became possible in some circumstances to purchase nominal membership in this class, with some social and legal effects that will be noted below.

The majority of the Korean population during the Yi period was termed the *yangin* ("good people") or *sangmin* ("ordinary people"); they were the common farmers and the addressees of tax, tribute, and military-service systems of the central government. Commoners actually in military service (rather than simply paying the alternative tax) were governed by distinct procedural provisions of the military statutes.

Below the commoners were the *ch'ŏnin* (the "despised people"), including slaves and those in demeaned occupations, such as butchers, prostitutes, entertainers, and shamans. Many petty functionaries of the

---

greater, the person is to be detained; where the person is a civil or military official, a palace attendant, a woman of a noble family or a monk, memorialize before detaining. . . . In a capital case, first detain then memorialize."

[69] See Yi Sang-baek, *Han'guksa: kunse chŏn'gip'yŏn* [*The History of Korea: Early Yi Period*] (Seoul: Ŭryu munhwasa, pp. 303–324. Kim Yŏng-mo, *Chosŏn chibaech'ŭng yŏn'gu*, notes the popularity of the three-part division used here. Both Yi and Kim discuss in some detail the complexities which such a classificatory scheme omits. Royal kin, for example, were legally distinguished from *yangban* and occupied a superior position in many situations. *Yangban* were also subdivided in various ways, depending on the rank of the office held, status as merit subjects, etc.

[70] Kim Yŏng-mo, *Chosŏn chibaech'ŭng yŏn'gu*, pp. 27–28, describes four types of *yangban*, including those with rank and office, those with rank and without office, those without rank but with office, and those with neither rank nor office. This is a logical scheme rather than a description of codified law, but it illustrates well the interaction between ascriptive factors and considerations of political or administrative authority.

government, such as postal-station employees or underlings of the county magistrates' yamen, were also classified as *ch'ŏnin*.

In principle, these three broad social categories were hereditary, a tradition which had economic and ideological implications. In reality, considerable slippage took place, as commoners illegally commended themselves as slaves to wealthy households in order to avoid taxation and labor-service duties, as slaves fled servitude and became indistinguishable from self-supporting commoners, and as individuals "dropped out" of *yangban* status through economic reversal or illegitimate birth. Efforts of the central government from the early decades of the Yi dynasty to check this slippage included census surveys, a "five-family-unit" system of registration (*oga chakt'ong*) on the model of the T'ang *pao chia* system, and a national identification-pass system (*hop'ae*).[71] None of these expedients seems to have been totally successful, and the central government never developed the tight control over local communities and social mobility that characterized Tokugawa rule in Japan.[72] A rigid and hierarchical social order supported by a strong legal structure remained more an aspiration than a concrete achievement of Yi dynasty government.

It may have been the inability of the government to create and maintain an airtight social caste system that accounted for repeated efforts on the part of members of the elite to artificially multiply the number of petty social and legal distinctions available, especially within the elite itself. Policy deliberations and legislative proposals often revealed a desire for finer gradations. One such debate in the early Yi period hinged on whether all members of the official class should observe ancestral rites for four generations of ancestors (following Ming practice and the *Family Rites* of Chu Hsi), or whether the official class itself should be divided into three ranked categories, with the high-level officials entitled to four generations of ritual observance, middle-level officials to three generations, and low-level officials to two. Following decades of debate and policy reversals, the more hierarchical practice was finally institutionalized in the late fifteenth century.[73]

The Yi-dynasty elite also departed from Chinese and earlier Korean practice in introducing discrimination against some of its own offspring

[71] Lee Kwang-nin, "Census Taking Under the Yi Dynasty," *Transactions of the Korea Branch of the Royal Asiatic Society*, 35 (1959), 47.

[72] Dieter Eikemeier, "Villages and Quarters as Instruments of Local Control in Yi Dynasty Korea," *T'oung Pao* [*Revue Internationale de Sinologie*], 62:1–3 (1976), 71–110. Eikemeier adds a great deal to our understanding of local government but reinforces this observation in the main.

[73] *Kyŏngguk taejŏn*, p. 276. The debates are discussed by Kim Tu-hŏn in *Han'guk kajok chedo yŏn'gu*, pp. 402–406. Kim points out that the debate was not closed even with the enactment of this code, for the four-generation system of the *Family Rites* seems to have become widely accepted over the following century with the diffusion of neo-Confucian thought.

through legislation prohibiting the sons of *yangban* and concubines from standing for the civil-service examination or serving in government posts.[74] Another group, the "middle people" (*chungin*), who played an important role in government as technical experts in language, accounting, law, and medicine, was also legally barred from policy-level posts.[75]

In the later Yi period, complaints were often heard that the broad social distinctions (*myŏngbun*) between elite and nonelite levels of society were collapsing. One late eighteenth-century official expressed the sentiments of many in a memorial to the throne:

> Impoverished and destitute nobility are made the butt of contumely and insult by commoners and lowborn. In the market places idle good-for-nothings shout out the names of state ministers. Village lowborn exceed their station in dress and food. The policy of first priority at this time must be to put distinctions of status in order and establish the institutional order.[76]

Evidence of similar dissatisfaction can be found across a broad spectrum of elite opinion, from high-ranking officials of the central government, to the writers of practical handbooks for county magistrates,[77] to out-of-office institutional critics.[78]

In summary, we find that the picture often presented of a legally buttressed hierarchical social order, while true in a general sense, must be qualified in several respects. First, the social categories of various types of Korean law—criminal statutes, census law, individual and household registration—were not entirely consistent in their details. There were also changes over time.[79] Furthermore, nearly constant fraud and evasion made even the general social structure embodied in the codes somewhat inaccurate as a portrayal of social reality. Finally, members of the elite desired (and sometimes created) far more ramified and varied intra-elite distinctions than the legal system could consistently provide. At the same time, members of the elite were dissatisfied with the level of enforcement

[74] Kim Yŏng-mo, *Chosŏn chibaech'ŭng yŏn'gu*, p. 40. Han Woo-keun, *The History of Korea* (Seoul: Eul-Yoo [Ŭryu munhwasa], 1970), p. 250.

[75] Han Woo-Keun, *The History of Korea,* p. 240. Edward W. Wagner, "An Inquiry into the *Chungin* Class in the Yi Dynasty," a paper given before the Columbia University Seminar on Korea, May 18, 1973.

[76] *Chŏngjo sillok, kwŏn* 2.60b–61a.

[77] Naitō Yoshinosuke, *Chōsen minsei shiryō* [Historical Materials on Local Governance in the Chosŏn Period] (Seoul: Naitō Yoshinosuke, 1942), p. 6, item 11; p. 225, item 15.

[78] Chŏng Sang-gi (1678–1752), *Nongp'o mundap*, p. 319.

[79] Kim Yŏng-mo, *Chosŏn chibaech'ŭng yŏn'gu*, p. 18.

of existing status boundaries. Thus it would be an error to suppose that traditional Korean law was a simple reflection of either the ascriptive categories of Korean culture or the social prejudices of members of the official class. Throughout the Yi period, society and law were never in a state of perfect congruence, but continued to interact with each other.

Legal reasoning as seen in case records provides a useful supplement to material contained in the codes and an excellent source for examining this interaction among the written law, official opinion, and Korean society. The complexity of this interaction may be seen in the two areas discussed below: the social position and judicial treatment of women, and the relationship between law and socioeconomic change in the later Yi period.

Women and the law—Given the unequal position of women in Confucian thought, in Korean culture, and in the law,[80] what can be learned from the cases about the ways in which women were treated by society and in judicial decisions? Were women more likely to be the victims of violence than men? Did judicial decisions follow the law or go beyond the statutes in imposing discriminatory judgments on women? Several generalizations can be made:

Women appeared only rarely as defendants in serious criminal cases. They were defendants in only two of the one hundred *simni* cases examined for this study, and they accounted for less than 2 percent of the defendants in a contemporary collection of less serious cases.[81] Reported

[80] The best treatment in English on the social and legal position of women in the Yi period is Martina Deuchler's "The Tradition: Women During the Yi Dynasty," in *Virtues in Conflict: Tradition and Korean Women Today*, ed. Sandra Mattielli (Seoul, Royal Asiatic Society, 1977), pp. 1–47. In Korean, see Ha Hyŏn-gang, "Chosŏn sidae [The Chosŏn Period]," in *Han'guk yŏsŏngsa* [*History of Korean Women*] (Seoul: Han'guk yŏsŏngsa p'yŏnch'an wiwŏnhoe [Committee for the Compilation of the History of Korean Women], 1972), I, 303–613. Jamie P. Horsley, "The Status of Woman in Traditional Chinese Law," unpublished third-year paper, Harvard Law School (1978), is a comprehensive treatment of Ch'ing legal provisions that would apply for the most part to Ming law as well. That the law in China and Korea dealt unequally with men and women cannot be denied. Several important qualifications should be noted, however, First, the law protected women (but not men) from certain kinds of violence. Sequestering of women, though not an unmixed blessing, may also have contributed to the apparently lower ratios of victimization of women noted in this study. Secondly, the position of Korean women with respect to some aspects of civil law, particularly property inheritance, was superior to that of women in Chinese law. Finally, it may be noted that considerations of gender were generally subordinated to considerations of hierarchy in both China and Korea. Thus, women were subordinated to men within given social strata and within the same generation of kin, but were sometimes superior legally and socially to men of a lower social stratum or generation.

[81] *Yullye yoram* [*Conspectus of Laws and Precedents*] (1837?), in *Sugyo chŏngnye —Yullye yoram* [*Received Edicts Enacted as Precedents—Conspectus of Laws and*

offenses were about evenly divided between sexual crimes and outbursts of jealousy and violence among wives and concubines.

If the *Simnirok* cases are an accurate reflection of over-all patterns of criminality, it would seem that men were not only more likely than women to commit crimes of violence in traditional Korea, but more likely to be victimized by crime as well. Only 25 percent of the homicide victims in the *Simnirok*, for example, were women. The fact that women were often discriminated against in the law does not seem to have encouraged violence against them. The physical isolation of women within the home, and other cultural factors, may also have contributed to this pattern. With respect to violent crime and homicide, it was far more dangerous to be a man than a woman in eighteenth-century Korea.

Violence between husband and wife is an area that deserves special comment. The violence of a husband against his wife was not a criminal matter under the Ming Code unless broken bones or more serious injuries resulted;[82] even then, the wife bore the burden of filing a formal complaint. Consequently, offenses of this sort may have been underreported. Nearly half of the women murder victims in the examined cases were killed by their husbands. The punishments meted out to husbands for this offense were invariably less than death, though within the general discretionary range of other *Simnirok* judgments.

Murder of a husband by his wife was not a common crime in the *Simnirok* records, but the dynastic annals for the seventeenth and eighteenth centuries cite a number of instances that came to the court for judgment.[83] A preliminary survey of these cases indicates that although most charges of wife-murder were reduced (as in the *Simnirok*) to manslaughter and the husbands given a reduced sentence, most wives charged with killing their husbands were given the death penalty. More effort also seems to have been spent in deliberation over the sentences of the male defendants. This would seem to be an area where a double standard of judgment clearly existed in traditional Korea, and where inequality in judgment went beyond the already unequal provisions of the criminal code.

Law and social change—The sense that the traditional system of status distinctions was eroding was partly the result of social and economic changes taking place in the seventeenth and eighteenth centuries.[84] In

Precedents] (Seoul: Pŏpchech'ŏ, 1970).

[82] *Taemyŏngnyul chikhae*, pp. 462–464.

[83] *Chosŏn wangjo sillok* [*Veritable Records of the Chosŏn Dynasty*], index vol., p. 346, under *salch'ŏjoe* [crime of murdering one's wife] and *salbujoe* [crime of murdering one's husband]; and p. 427, under *sibujoein* [women who murdered their husbands].

[84] Susan Shin, "The Social Structure of Kumhwa County in the Late Seventeenth

some communities, industrious farmers of commoner or lower status were using new financial and managerial techniques to produce commercial crops and improve their economic position, while the position of less efficient local *yangban* landowners remained static or deteriorated to a situation of genteel poverty.[85] Purchase of nominal elite status had been possible since the late sixteenth-century Japanese invasions, when the government sought to replenish state coffers by the selling of titles (*napsok*). Such limited "mobility" did not affect national political life,[86] but could contribute to the gradual weakening of status lines in affected rural areas, as those who within living memory had been commoners or lowborn villagers became able to purchase titles, gain exemption from taxes, "persuade" census clerks to change their registration, or purchase forged genealogical pedigrees.[87] Economic distinctions were coming to rival those based on traditional status considerations.

Other changes were taking place at the lower edge of village society. As many commoners fled tax burdens by purchasing titles, by surreptitiously registering as slaves,[88] or in other ways, the government encouraged wealthy slaves to purchase their way out of hereditary servitude (*songnyang*) and changed the laws on inheritance of slave status to allow more offspring of slave-commoner marriages to escape upward into commoner status.[89] The growing importance of contract and short-term wage labor (especially for the new entrepreneurial farming) also diminished the economic importance of slavery. The effects of all these developments on the national economy are still largely unstudied. It is clear, however, that when such developments occurred at the local level they could have a corrosive effect on ascriptive status distinctions and contribute to the growing feeling of the Yi-dynasty elite that those beneath them in the traditional scheme of things were losing their sense of station. The criminal-case records contain numerous instances of individuals brought to trial for acts of enraged violence in reaction to the contumacious or insubordinate behavior and language of wage laborers, former slaves, or the commoner husbands of slave women.

Century," *Occasional Papers on Korea*, No. 1, revised edition (April, 1974), pp. 12–15.

[85] Kim Yong-sŏp, *Chosŏn hugi nongŏpsa yŏn'gu* [*Studies in the Agrarian History of the Later Yi Dynasty*], I (Seoul: Ilchogak, 1970), 406–407; II (1971), 223–226.

[86] Kim Yŏng-mo, *Chosŏn chibaech'ŭng yŏn'gu*, pp. 45–46.

[87] Kim Yong-sŏp, *Chosŏn hugi nongŏpsa yŏn'gu*, II, 197–210.

[88] James B. Palais, *Politics and Policy in Traditional Korea* (Cambridge, Mass.: Harvard University Press, 1976), pp. 90–91.

[89] Hiraki Makoto, "Jūshichi-hachi seiki ni okeru doryōsai shosei no kizoku ni tsuite [Reversion of Status of Offspring of Slaves and Commoner Wives in the Seventeenth and Eighteenth Centuries]," *Chōsen gakuhō*, No. 61 (October, 1971), pp. 45–76.

These developments raised significant questions for legal administration and social policy. For example, what should be the moral and legal obligations of a former slave to a former master? Could an indentured laborer on a long-term contract, traditionally slavelike in status, be forcibly disciplined as a slave? What about short-term or casual labor? Did the commoner husbands of female slaves who lived in the household of the master enjoy the same protections against assault as the "ordinary person" of the statutes? Did *yangban* have any legal entitlement to the use of force in redressing insulting behavior from these technical commoners, or did they have to tolerate it? New legislation to deal with these and similar problems could provide a stopgap solution, arbitrarily treating the commoner husbands of slaves, for example, as if they were slaves in some situations while leaving them nearly as protected as commoners in others.[90] But the result was to move even further away from the vision of a legal system that unambiguously and systematically supported the traditional class structure of Korean society. *Yangban* aspirations for a closer fit between law and society increasingly foundered on the twin shoals of changing social reality and the momentum of the law itself toward rationality and inner consistency.

Conclusion

Chinese and Korean statutory law gave legal and institutional force to a premise—profound and pervasive social inequality—that is radically distinct from the premises underlying "modern" legal thought and institutions.[91] In examining the interaction of law and society, however, it is not sufficient simply to ask whether the written codes contained inequalities. Judicial decisions should also be studied to see how the laws were applied in practice. A legal system in which codified inequalities are administered consistently and "rationally" may be quite different from a legal system without formal limits to the subjective whims or social prejudices of the judges.[92] The question of which kind of legal system oper-

[90] *Sugyo chŏngnye*, pp. 93–97.

[91] The perspective of a social scientist is given by Marc Galanter, "The Modernization of Law," in *Modernization*, ed. Myron Weiner (New York: 1966), pp. 153–165. Galanter coins the term "transactional" to describe the act-orientation of modern law. By this criterion, Chinese and Korean law, which also took the age, sex, status, and other characteristics of the person into account, could not be described as modern. Chinese and Korean law did, however, exemplify many of the other marks of "modernity" that Galanter cites.

[92] Max Weber found it useful to distinguish between "substantive rationality" and "substantive irrationality" in analyzing types of law and legal decision-making. Both types involve the intrusion of extralegal norms—in this case, considerations of social status—into the law, but the former does so on a systematic basis, allowing at least for predictability and the possibility of checks upon abuses. For a con-

ated in traditional Korea takes on additional significance in the light of oft-expressed elite dissatisfaction with the decay of customary social categories and constant efforts by members of a status-conscious elite to multiply categories of privilege.

What do the cases reveal about the effect of social status considerations on judicial decisions? Did legal officials confine themselves to the built-in inequalities of the code, or did they push social inequality even further as their personal feelings inclined them? How committed were they to rule by law? Exceptions to the principle of legality may of course be found. There seems to have been a double standard of clemency, for example, with respect to murder of a spouse, because women were almost always given the full penalty, while men were almost always awarded a reduced sentence. Formal legal protection from assault seems to have meant little where the victim was a butcher, for example, or a beggar, or some other member of a virtually outcast group. Judicial authorities found it difficult to regard enraged and violent responses to insults from such persons as really culpable, no matter what the law said. Even in these instances, however, such offenses *were* prosecuted and not simply disregarded. Legal reasoning may have yielded to social rationalization in the final disposition of such cases, but the law was not a cipher.

Despite these exceptional cases, the law seems generally to have been upheld. Officials and *yangban* were prosecuted, tried (often with the routine use of torture in interrogation), and punished for acts of violence against a variety of nonelite persons ranging from shopkeepers to day laborers and former slaves. Thus, although the social ethos of Yi-dynasty elite society held it to be far worse for crimes to be committed upward than downward (and this view had the support of the law), the law successfully imposed limits and did not permit crimes against social inferiors with impunity.

LOCAL SOCIETY AND GOVERNMENT IN EIGHTEENTH-CENTURY KOREA

Case records not only reveal patterns of legal reasoning and thought but provide a wealth of information about the nature of local society and government. No "police-blotter" account can give a total or well-rounded picture of a society. Nonetheless, such records do contain valuable information often not accessible elsewhere and help to provide both an immediacy and a balance sometimes missing from other records of a more secondary nature. The *Simnirok* cases are especially informative where they touch on the role of violence in rural life, attitudes toward involve-

venient summary of this model, see Max Rheinstein, "Introduction," in *Max Weber on Law in Economy and Society*, trans. Max Rheinstein and Edward Shils (New York: Simon and Schuster, 1967), pp. xxxix–xliv.

ment with the law, and the nature and quality of local government. Examination of these areas may result in the reexamination of some of the generalizations and suppositions commonly held concerning traditional Korean rural society.

Violence

Since the *simni* hearings were primarily concerned with homicide cases, or with cases purported to be homicides, *simni* records reveal a great deal about the nature and role of violence in rural Korean life in the late eighteenth century. Case records for less serious crimes found in other contemporary sources show similar patterns and indicate that the *Simnirok* records may be taken as broadly indicative of the general sociology of crime in Korea at that time.[93]

The society revealed by the criminal case records is that of rural Korea. Disputes occur over the staple concerns of village life. Irrigation rights, a plot of burial land, the theft of a draft animal, an altercation with in-laws—all of these might occasion disagreement, quarreling, and sometimes fatal violence. The tools of village life—a grain sickle, a fodder knife, a shovel handle—could provide the occasion or the means for violent assault. For many individuals appearing in these records, the conditions of life appear to have been stringent or even marginal. Tempers flared over petty or imagined issues, the frustrations of a quarrel were sometimes taken out on bystanders, and poor health often conspired to convert a moderate injury into a mortal one. Thus the case records indicate that violence—whether resulting in culpable homicide or not—occurred within the context of village routine rather than as a violation of that routine.

A variety of motives for quarrels and interpersonal violence are suggested in the records. Sexual misconduct was a common cause of assault and homicide. Theft or suspicion of theft of household objects, animals, or land records might easily escalate into violence. Debts, money, and taxes played a role in some violent disputes, reflecting both rural stringency and partial monetization of the economy at that time. Self-help to avenge an injury or an insult suffered by a relative was not uncommon, encouraged by Confucian piety and countenanced by lenient code provisions.[94] But violence *against* near relatives or in-laws was even more common, despite legal disincentives and Confucian moralizing.

Several features of rural society combined to exacerbate the normal

[93] *Yullye yoram* [*Conspectus of Laws and Precedents*] (1837?), in *Sugyo chŏngnye—Yullye yoram* [*Received Edicts Enacted as Precedents—Conspectus of Laws and Precedents*] (Seoul: Pŏpchech'ŏ, 1970).

[94] For cases, see Pak Il-wŏn, ed., *Ch'ugwanji*, pp. 211–238. The topic is touched on by Lu Shiu-Lian in "A Comparative Study of the American and Chinese Law of Justifiable Defense," *Chengchi Law Review*, 6 (June, 1972), 293–350.

tensions and severe material conditions of life and livelihood. Alcohol appears in the case records as a catalyst of disorder and violence and as a contributory factor in the demise of several assault victims. Drunkenness sometimes led to exchanges of insults, followed by blows. The attitude of governmental authorities toward alcohol was ambivalent. Periodic prohibitions on the production and consumption of wine (*kŭmju*) were based on awareness of the social cost of excessive drinking as well as on considerations of seasonal agronomy; spring wine-making could exhaust stores of seed grain with disastrous results.[95] Such prohibitions and the accompanying pronouncements were generally honored more in the breach than in the observance. Meanwhile, in legal decisions, medical guidelines of the coroners's handbook (*Muwŏllok*)[96] were followed in treating a victim's drunkenness as a contributory cause of death, lessening the culpability of the defendant. A defendant's drunkenness might also give insight into his state of mind and serve as grounds for partial exoneration.

Village gossip also played a significant and provocative role in rural violence, especially in instances of assault by a suspicious or enraged husband against his wife or her rumored paramour. The Ming Code sanctioned vengeance only when the husband discovered his wife *in flagrante*; it did not treat hearsay or gossip as sufficient evidence to justify self-help.[97] The cases show more instances of the latter than the former, however. Village rumor, like alcohol, was also a potent solvent of social status lines, adding infuriatingly specific details to the more general mockery of upper-class manners and morals so popular in peasant drama and other folk entertainments.[98]

Attitudes Toward Involvement with the Law

Some accounts of traditional Chinese law suggest that most people sought to avoid involvement with the courts and with the legal process at all costs.[99] This was true for Korea only with some qualifications. It scarcely applies at all, for example, with respect to civil suits. Available records from the early part of the Yi period on through the seventeenth and eighteenth centuries indicate that where land, slave ownership, or gravesite plots in particular were at stake, Koreans of all classes possessed a

95 (*Chŭngpo*) *Munhŏn pigo*, vol. III, *kwŏn* 131.

96 *Chŭngsu muwŏllok* [*Amplified and Corrected Coroner's Guide for the Elimination of Grievances*], Pŏpchech'ŏ pŏpche charyo ch'ilsipp'al chip [vol. 78 of the Office of Legislation series of legal source materials] (Seoul: Pŏpchech'ŏ, 1975).

97 *Taemyŏngnyul chikhae*, pp. 539–540.

98 Yi Tu-hyŏn, *Han'guk kamyŏn'guk* [*Korean Mask Dance Drama*] (Seoul: Han'guk kamyŏn'guk yŏn'guhoe, 1969).

99 See Derk Bodde and Clarence Morris, *Law in Imperial China*, p. 173.

strong sense of entitlement and in fact "loved to litigate" (*hosong*).[100] The hope of having one's case heard and one's grievance eased produced a flood of petitioners; and institutions for handling such litigation, from the county magistrate's office on up through various special appeal facilities such as the petition drum outside the royal palace in the capital, were virtually overloaded with petitioners bringing all manner of complaints, appeals, and suits.[101] Many of those bringing civil complaints urged that their opponents be charged with criminal offenses for good measure.[102]

Most people were not so eager to become involved in a criminal case, however, even as witnesses. Torture of witnesses as well as suspects was a common feature of criminal investigations, and did not always proceed according to regulation. Doubtless yamen underlings, as in China, also took advantage of the opportunities provided by an ongoing investigation to turn a personal profit from time to time. The financial and personal risks of involvement in a criminal case were therefore considerable, and the hope of gain present in a civil dispute was absent altogether.

However, when a quarrel or fight resulted in the death of someone and an investigation was opened, it was difficult for relatives of the suspect and the victim to avoid involvement with the law. One tactic available to forestall an investigation was agreement between the assailant and the family of the deceased for the former to make amends and for both sides to prevent the authorities from getting wind of the exact circumstances of the victim's demise. The motivation of a potential suspect in a murder trial for such an arrangement need not be further probed. What is less obvious is that the family of the deceased also had reasons for hoping to settle privately. The physical and financial risks of involvement in a murder investigation have been mentioned above. To these must be added the indignity of having the deceased undergo at least two inquest autopsies, and possibly also a disinterment autopsy some months or years after the body had been buried. There were thus some situations, particularly where the death may have been accidental or unintentional, in which the offer of burial expenses would have seemed an attractive alternative to the length, uncertainty, and risks of a legal battle.

---

[100] *Taejŏn hoet'ong* [*Second Composite Edition of Great Code and Supplements*] (1865) (Keijō [Seoul]: Chōsen sōtokufu chūsūin, 1939), pp. 697–699. The legislative history of many of these provisions attempting to cope with Korean litigiousness extends back to the sixteenth and seventeenth centuries.

[101] Ibid. See also Han U-gŭn, "Sinmun'go ŭi sŏlch'i wa kŭ silchaejŏk hyonŭng e taehayŏ [A Study of the Establishment of the Petition Drum System and Its Effectiveness]," in *Yi Pyŏng-do paksa hwagap kinyŏm nonch'ong* [*Festschrift in Honor of the Sixtieth Birthday of Dr. Yi Pyŏng-do*] (Seoul: Ilchogak, 1956), pp. 357–408.

[102] Pak Pyŏng-ho, *Han'guk pŏpchesago* [*Studies in Korean Legal History*] (Seoul: Pŏmmunsa, 1974), p. 251.

This kind of agreement was not without its own risks for both parties. Confucian propriety and statutory law encouraged the cultivation of a spirit of vengeance, not reconciliation, toward anyone insulting or injuring a close kinsman. Relatives of such a victim were supposed to feel "unable to share the same sky" (*pulgong taech'ŏn*) with the assailant. Where major crimes like homicide were suspected, the state in China and Korea also naturally sought to maximize its participation and to extend the reach of the law and the legal process as far into the countryside as possible, both to exert its own authority and to confront and preempt all rival powers and modes of adjudication at the local level. The Ming Code embodied both the ideological and institutional imperatives by criminalizing "private settlement" (*sahwa*). Moreover, judicial decisions commonly reflected the conviction that an offer of burial expenses was *prima facie* evidence of guilt on the part of a defendant, whether or not the offer was accepted and technical charges of "private settlement" could be pressed. For the most part, these legal and ideological pressures seem to have been effective in limiting the incidence of "private settlement," although not in eliminating it entirely.

Knowledge of the popular attitude toward involvement in criminal matters could sometimes help judicial authorities in their investigations. For example, an otherwise uninvolved person who "came forward" to volunteer helpful suggestions to the investigators could arouse suspicion of his own motives. As in the case of Yi Ka-wŏn (see Appendix), such a person might be trying to stir up legal difficulties for others as part of an extortion attempt. In traditional Korea, blackmail using the threat of legal involvement was apparently open to freelance operators as well as to the professionals from the magistrate's office.

Relatives of a suspected murder victim, on the other hand, could be helpful in exonerating a suspect if they voluntarily showed that they bore no grudge or if they passed along deathbed testimony favorable to the defendant. Negative testimony from the deceased's kin was expected (and discounted accordingly); favorable remarks from this quarter could be helpful in assessing the defendant's degree of culpability and intent.

A third type of voluntary legal involvement that had important implications for a criminal investigation was the coming forward of a relative of the accused to submit a petition for his release. Local officials discouraged such petitions because they invariably led to troublesome reinvestigations. There were risks for the petitioner, including the likelihood that he would undergo torture in any follow-up investigation and the near certainty of penal sanctions for false allegations in such a petition. On the other hand, those who braved these and other obstacles would be assured that their appeal would be taken seriously. The king and high-level officials rarely failed to be impressed by the commitment and courage of honest petitioners; in a significant number of instances, such petitions contributed to a reduced sentence or outright acquittal of the accused.

The Quality of Local Government

On the basis of the case records contained in the *Simnirok* and other collections, it seems that Korean judicial administration–at least at the higher levels of government, and at least where death penalty cases were concerned–was more subject to the principle of legality and less subject to the arbitrary whim of the authorities than has hitherto been supposed. It should be recalled, however, that the *simni* process itself originated in efforts of the central government to adjudicate "unjustly handled cases" (*wŏnok*). In the early part of the Yi period, officials called *simnisa* were dispatched to the provinces on the suspicion, no doubt justified, that local administration of justice sometimes fell below the desired standard. Regularization of the *simni* process under King Chŏngjo (r. 1776–1800) reveals that the need for such review of local incompetence or malfeasance persisted. Thus some of the *simni* cases shed light on the nature and extent of problems in the administration of law at the local levels of Korean government. These problems can be broadly divided into two categories: willful corruption by manipulation of the laws, and malfeasance brought about by ignorance or incompetence.

Corruption

According to contemporary critiques willful corruption was an everpresent problem in Korean local government. Clerks and underlings were often singled out for blame, because they functioned as intermediaries between the county magistrate and village-level society and had numerous opportunities to "skin" (*pakhal*) the populace by falsification of the labor-service rosters,[103] improper drafting of legal documents for illiterate peasants,[104] or in numerous other ways. Korean codes from the fifteenth century contained a chapter entitled "vicious functionaries" (*wŏnak hyangi*) enumerating the possibilities.[105] As has been noted above, one of the arguments advanced for legal reform in the eighteenth century was that statutory inconsistencies made it that much easier for corrupt functionaries to manipulate the laws to their own profit. King Chŏngjo himself once used a popular phrase in referring to the law as "soft deerskin" (*sungnokp'i taejŏn*) that could be stretched in any direction by the unscrupulous.[106]

About 5 percent of the *simni* cases concerned the forgery of state seals by petty officials. The case records show that there was a market in forged documents that might be used by government functionaries in their

[103] Naitō Yoshinosuke, *Chōsen minsei shiryō*, p. 81, item 19.

[104] *Taejŏn hoet'ong*, pp. 679–680.

[105] *Kyŏngguk taejŏn*, pp. 478–479.

[106] *Ilsŏngnok palch'we* (*pŏpchŏn*) [*Selections from the Ilsŏngnok* (*legal codes*)], p. 107b.

efforts to extort money from the hapless populace—"encroaching upon the fish" (*ch'im'ŏ*), to use the contemporary term:

> This man, who was a runner, had taken to wearing the identity tag of a guardsman and was performing other duties than his own [Case #20].
>
> Using the pretext of official orders, they make demands upon the village people; not content to extort and intimidate, they even tie and beat them [Case #455].
>
> This forgery of state seals and the manufacture and sale of some one hundred [spurious] documents are truly unpardonable capital offenses [Case #125].[107]

Central-government concern over this kind of problem undoubtedly accounts for the haste with which forgery cases were handled in comparison with other death-penalty offenses. Of the cases examined for this study, 60 percent required from one to four years for a decision, while most forgery cases were decided within less than one year.

Legal Competency at the Local Level

A major purpose of the *simni* hearings was to reexamine the investigative records to ascertain whether grounds for clemency might be found. Part of this reexamination required careful scrutiny of the reports filed by the county magistrate at the time of the inquest. On the whole, magistrates seem to have competently followed the technical procedures of the coroner's manual. In some cases, however, the king or high officials taking part in the *simni* hearing found fault with the level of expertise and overturned the findings of the inquest investigation.

In some cases, local officials were disciplined for incompetent conduct of the inquest investigation; in other cases they were simply reprimanded. In one such case, the king criticized the fact that the inquest official had superficially concluded that the deceased had died from internal injuries:

> They pinned it on internal injuries since they could find no external wounds. But the way in which this was done does not correspond to the provisions of the *Muwŏllok* pertaining to internal injuries, and must be put down to simple speculation on the part of the inquest officials. [This] is a grave violation of the policy of careful investigation.[108]

---

[107] *Simnirok*, I, 8, 332, 61.

[108] Ibid., p. 213.

No disciplinary steps seem to have been taken in this case. In the case of Yi Ka-wŏn (# 145), however, two magistrates were disciplined for incompetence in conducting the inquest, and the provincial governor was removed from his post. In dismissing the governor, the king cited numerous inconsistencies in the depositions and other suspicious circumstances surrounding the case, which the governor had overlooked in his investigations.

Conclusion

Society–It would seem that Korean rural society was not fully self-administrating. There appears to have been constant legal interaction between the central government and the county level, dictated both by the occurrence of sporadic interpersonal violence and by more systematic efforts of locally influential persons or corrupt yamen underlings to abuse their power at the expense of weaker members of the community. County-level administrators freely and directly entered village communities to conduct inquest and other investigative hearings; and peasants often brought village-level problems to the attention of the central government through the established lines of appeal.

Instances of serious crime disclose, in exaggerated form, undercurrents of tension that must have been constantly present in village life. Brought about by the difficult conditions of livelihood and the stresses of in-law and other human relationships, including conflict with "local magnates," and exacerbated by village gossip and drinking, these tensions and undercurrents qualify the picture sometimes drawn of "village harmony."[109] The occurrence of interpersonal violence of a more or less serious kind, often over immediate petty issues, also provides indirect evidence that institutions of conflict mediation–supposedly a major aspect of village life in China[110]–may have been weak and ineffective in traditional Korea.

Legal Involvement

The relative weakness of informal institutions of mediation at the village level is also suggested by the willingness of villagers to make use of state-provided appeal mechanisms for expressing civil and criminal grievances. Such appeals persisted despite psychological and legal barriers and an element of risk. Peasant awareness of the law may have been

[109] Vincent Brandt, *A Korean Village: Between Farm and Sea* (Cambridge, Mass: Harvard University Press, 1971). Brandt usefully distinguishes between "hierarchical" and "egalitarian-cooperative" social patterns but pays relatively little attention to conflict.

[110] Sybille van der Sprenkel, *Legal Institutions in Manchu China* (New York: Humanities Press, 1966). Jerome Alan Cohen, "Chinese Mediation on the Eve of Modernization," *California Law Review*, 54:2 (August, 1966), 1201–1226.

marginal at best, but peasant social and institutional horizons were not limited to the sphere of village life;[111] villagers readily made use of national mechanisms to protest injustice and seek remedies. If "rights consciousness" is an inappropriate characterization for peasant willingness to petition, neither may peasants be portrayed as limited to abject subjugation, on the one hand, or violent rebellion, on the other.

Local government—The cases help round out a picture of the quality of local legal administration by shedding light on official, semiofficial, and nonofficial abuse of power at the local level. Though local abuse of power may have remained a problem more often exposed than corrected during this period, the central government appears at least to have placed a high priority on the punishment of counterfeiting and abuse of official seals and documents. Elapsed time between the filing of charges and sentencing was far shorter for such cases than for the murder cases contained in the *simni* collection. Instances of local officials being disciplined for incompetence or malfeasance in the conduct of criminal investigations also reflect the concern of the central-government authorities for establishing uniform standards of local judicial administration. The *simni* procedure itself, however, testifies to the persistence of less than adequate levels of legal acumen, competence, and integrity at the local levels of government.

APPENDIX: THE CASE OF CHO CHAE-HANG (YI KA-WŎN)

[Author's note: This case is one of 100 translated and examined in my larger study *Legal Norms in a Confucian State* (to be published by the Institute of East Asian Studies in its Korea Research Monograph series). The document from which these cases were representatively selected is the *Shimnirok*, a late 18th century compilation of serious cases under review at the royal court in Korea. Case decisions in the *Shimnirok* were to have the status of judicial precedents and were to be "respectfully observed" by legal officials in subsequent trials.]

Case of Cho Chae-hang
Hwanghae Province
Paekch'ŏn County
Case filed: 1780.6
Final entry: 1783.6
Conclusion: "released"

[111] Leon Stover, *The Cultural Ecology of Chinese Civilization: Peasants and Elites*

Chae-hang struck and kicked his wife, Yun's daughter, over a bowl of food. She died the same day. The inquest determined the cause of death to be kicking. The case was filed in 1780.6 (*Simnirok* [henceforth *SR*], 1.75–76).

In the first *simni* hearing (1780.12), the governor's report memorial commented on the defendant's attempt to hide the evidence of the wounds by delaying the burial for five days. The Board of Punishments declined to comment on the case since the king had ordered a special investigation (*sa*). The king in his comments raised a number of suspicious and problematic aspects of the case to be found in the depositions collected from the defendant and relatives of the deceased: "The 'true cause' of death is the main thing to be considered, but testimonies must be in complete order before the case is formally filed. This is what safeguards life." Among the problems listed by the king were the unlikely shape of the wounds, the unfounded character of the stories in many of the depositions, tracing back to a female slave who by law was too young to be forcibly interrogated, the failure of one suspicious individual who examined the body to examine the back of the victim, and the offer of a maternal cousin, Cho Kyŏng, to pay funeral costs instead of reporting the death immediately and directly.

In the light of these problems, the king was strongly critical of the local inquest officials and of the poor supervision exercised by the governor: "For the investigative officials to fail to reinvestigate these accusations and for the governor to continue to remain silent, thereby making Chae-hang the principal culprit and then lightly filing a report memorial–this is a major breakdown in the policy of careful consideration of cases. The groundless speculation and overhasty decision of the investigating officials are culpable. Let the proper agency [the State Tribunal?] try the director of the first inquest, the Paekch'ŏn magistrate Kwŏn Chung-nip, and the director of the second inquest, the magistrate of Yŏnan, Yi U-bae. As for the governor, he should be disciplined, taking into account aggravating circumstances, but for the time being let him appoint special investigative officers and reinvestigate the case in every way, then submit a report again."

In the second *simni* hearing (1781.8), the governor's investigation memorial (*sagye*) reasserted the validity of the original inquest findings: the wounds, regardless of their leaflike shape, were just like fatal kick wounds, and there could be no doubt that requital for a life was required. The Board of Punishments, however, citing the deliberate sowing of rumors concerning the killing, recommended in its response memorial

---

in the Last of the Agrarian States (New York: Pica Press, 1974). This ranks as the most extreme statement to date of the Redfieldian "two cultures" approach to Chinese society. For better or worse, Yi dynasty peasants have yet to receive the Western scholarly attention that has been devoted to their Chinese counterparts.

that questioning of Chae-hang be discontinued and that Pae's daughter be severely interrogated. The king approved the recommendation (*SR*, 1.131).

Chae-hang's younger brother, Chae-jŏng, petitioned (*kyŏkchaeng*) for the release of Chae-hang (*SR*, 1.173–174).

In the third *simni* hearing (1782.7), the board cast doubt on the validity of Chae-jŏng's petition, but recommended that the scope of the investigation be enlarged to include the interrogation of other local people. The king commented on the ambiguity of the injuries and the untrustworthiness of the witnesses' testimony and singled out two individuals in particular who had drawn suspicion upon themselves by their actions. Then, noting that the newly appointed head of the Board of Punishments had formerly been governor of Hwanghae Province, the king entrusted the investigation and *simni* records to him for a decision (*kyŏlch'ŏ*). The younger brother's petition was rejected, and he was ordered sent home pending the disposition of the matter by the royal court.

In the fourth *simni* hearing (1782.7), the board recommended that a number of the depositions taken be dismissed from consideration as "well-and-kitchen tales," and requested the interrogation of Yi Ka-wŏn, one of the individuals whose actions had aroused royal suspicion earlier. The king ordered Yi Ka-wŏn remanded to the provincial governor for incarceration at the provincial yamen lockup (*yŏngok*) pending a final decision, and ordered the board to consider further whether or not the original defendant, Chae-hang, should be judged leniently "in consideration of circumstances."

In the fifth and final *simni* hearing (1783.6), the governor reported (*SR*, 18 *kwon* text, 15.70a) in his investigation memorial (*sagye*) that Yi Ka-wŏn had fabricated charges and that Cho Kyŏng had received [a bribe?] and given a false deposition, for which an appropriate statute existed. The response memorial of the board added that both Yi Ka-wŏn and Cho Kyŏng should be severely judged and that the defendant Chae-hang should be "judged leniently in consideration" (*SR*, 1.225–27).

Royal Comment (*p'an*)—"When We examined the report memorial in this case in the *simni* hearing in the spring of 1781 [in the second *simni* hearing above], We noted a great preponderance of dubious material. We could have come to a quick decision and overturned the original recommendation, but given the seriousness of this case, it was difficult to take the short way and render a speculative judgment. Thus We handed down orders for repeated investigations. In the past three [*sic*] years, investigations have been carried out four times. To date, the capital officials have concentrated on the matter, and the provincial governor's investigation memorials have advanced a stage in exposing the wicked intentions of Yi Ka-wŏn and virtually exonerated [the original defendant] Chae-hang. For the guilty one to be caught and the innocent to be enabled to get off is a brilliant exemplification of the heavenly principle.

"In general, the rules for solving a case are not to be found apart from conventional common sense. When Yun's daughter died, and before any of the women in the neighboring community had uttered a single word of suspicion about the matter, Ka-wŏn butted into the affair and began to express his opinions. Chae-p'ung came forward to report the matter at once, without [even] putting on his hat, even though he was only related by marriage, out of a spirit of mutual aid and helpfulness. Ka-wŏn, however, dared at this time to nurse bad feelings and build up resentment and figured that he could make trouble for others with this incident.

"He began before the corpse was even cool to see this as an opportunity and began to check the body from head to foot in search of likely-looking injuries. When he could find nothing suspicious with which to carry out his plan, he began to broadcast the story about [someone] offering to pay the burial expenses, attempting to [extort] some money, but the money was not forthcoming and the body was buried. Then he began to formulate all kinds of speculations and racked his brains to make up several farmer's songs, which he first spread around among the farmers' wives. Then he incited the invalid Cho Kyŏng to call in I-bong . . . and report the charges to the officials a full forty days after the incident. During the six months while the inquests were being conducted, while they were having to search for injuries amid rotting flesh and very uncertain places, he was able to produce as a witness [to the presumed misdeed] only an ignorant child, so [the inquest officials had] no one to ask their questions of. His evil scheme to bring legal charges under way, he now began to think of bringing ruin to the whole family. . . . No one can know whether this was out of grievance over the death of a fifth-degree niece or because his scheme to make some money on the affair had miscarried.

"When at the instance of the throne an investigation began into the hidden circumstances of the matter, he reintensified his wickedness of heart and in haste began to falsely produce as witnesses many people who had not previously appeared in [the records of] the first or second inquests. . . .With all the directions and instructions he was giving, however, he was unable to prevent inconsistencies from arising. [For example], he painstakingly incited P'ung-hang to give the story that the defendant kicked the victim in the kitchen; P'ung-hang lived in another place, however, and was not clear on the details. Stories of [what happened by] the well blossomed like flowers, but no one was able to remember who they had been dipping water with that day. In sum, not only were everyone's depositions inconsistent, but all these tales got traced back to his [Ka-wŏn's?] wife. The bloody garments were conveniently nowhere to be found, and it was impossible to conceal the many dubious aspects of the whole thing.

“The most grievous aspect of the matter was the business of the farmer’s song. At the very beginning of his plans, he fabricated a ditty in vulgar [i.e., colloquial] speech and taught it to the village girls in an attempt to deceive and mislead general opinion. For each one who sang it, ten more would [hear it and] sing along, whether in the fields or along the pathways. Investigators from the county seat and casual passers-by alike would ask about the affair and in sympathy take [this account] for the truth. . . . However, [true] rural songs spring, as it were, from the fundaments of heaven as songs of mountain flower or field. . . . Commonly they seem simple at first but are actually difficult to understand. None of them are as explicit–as if in fear that people would not get the meaning–as the one in this case. If one had a knowledgeable person listen to them, he would be able to spot the fabrication immediately, and easily see that he tried a little too hard.

“As for the injuries, how can there be wounds worthy of the name with no trace of blood, or kicked places without circular [bruises]? The white flesh did turn blue-green, but there was never any purple and therefore no hemorrhaging. The plum-leaf shape became a bean-leaf shape, but these were leaf-shaped bruises, not circular. How can we file a case without [evidence of] hemorrhaging or circular bruises? According to the methods of the *Muwŏllok*, a genuine injury will remain bluish or reddish, then quickly turn white; but in this instance, we have a white place with no prior redness. It was a major error of investigation to decide that it was an injury on the basis of appearance alone, without going into the question of whether the [required] changes had taken place.

“The so-called ‘water method,’ where water is poured from above and a wound is detected by noting where the water does not run off, must be conducted and observed before inquest can be regarded as complete. But in the concluding summary of both inquest reports, the question of damage was not mentioned; rather the words ‘the poured water did not run off’ alone appeared, leaving the impression that the water method had been used. This was a serious oversight. The two inquest officials can escape their culpability in this matter only with difficulty, but there is no point in going into this again at this time, since they were already investigated and disciplined last year. However, We do not dare to be casual in Our examination of the documents pertaining to a murder case, due to Our concern for circumspect integrity.

“. . . Though We ordered investigations, [the governor] did not undertake an examination in person, but relegated the matter to the magistrate. After a hurried and superficial inquiry, the memorial was sent up again, as previously. What is worse, inconsistent stories, not even worth making use of as a temporary expedient, were relied upon, causing the case to be delayed with the resultant evils and limitless scheming. If there hadn’t been further investigation, Ka-wŏn’s wicked intentions would have gone undiscovered and Chae-hang's grievance would not have been requited. Could there have been an inversion of criminal administration greater than this? It was not possible to simply leave the matter as decided just because the incident was over and done with. Have the governor Cho Sang-jin relieved of his post.

"As for Ka-wŏn's crime of scheming over a corpse and falsely accusing another of murder, appropriate statutes exist. However, since Chae-hang has not yet been condemned to death, Ka-wŏn likewise should 'take his place before the law' (*panjwa*) [and may get off without being executed.[1]]. Beat Ka-wŏn severely and, reducing his sentence from death to banishment to a fixed place, send him to a remote frontier for life. Cho Kyŏng's sympathy with Ka-wŏn is most grievous; however, he was an accomplice, not [the principal offender] like Ka-wŏn. Let his sentence be reduced from death and have him sentenced to labor service (*tobae*). The other individuals merely followed along blindly and are all foolish simpletons; let them be sentenced according to their degree of culpability.

"As for the defendant in the murder case from Paekch'ŏn County, Cho Chae-hang, he may not be confined any longer now that his innocence is known. Explain this judgment to him clearly and release him (*pangsong*)."

William Shaw is Research Associate in East Asian Legal Studies at the Harvard Law School. His recent and forthcoming publications include *Legal Norms in a Confucian State*, Korea Research Monograph No. 5 (forthcoming); "Traditional Korean Law and its Relation to China" in *China's Legal Tradition*, edited by Jerome A. Cohen, R. Randle Edwards, and Fu-mei Ch'en (Princeton: Princeton University Press, 1980); and "The Neo-Confucian Revolution of Values in Early Yi Korea and its Implications for Legal Thought" in *Law and State in Traditional East Asia*, edited by Brian McKnight (Honolulu: University of Hawaii Press). Dr. Shaw is currently studying Korean social and intellectual trends of the 1920s.

[1] Although Ka-wŏn's sentence differs slightly from that provided by the Ming Code in accordance with Korean banishment practice, the principle that a false accuser should not be executed if his intended victim had not actually been sentenced follows the code. *Taemyŏngnyul chikhae* pp. 445–451. The statute is cited in a similar case in the Board of Punishment records; *Ch'ugwanji*, p. 832.

Development of Law and Legal Institutions in Korea

Dai-kwon Choi

THE ISSUES

Since the end of the Yi dynasty in 1910 two decisive events have occurred in the development of Korean law. First the institutions of traditional Korea were suddenly replaced, under Japanese rule, by Western legal institutions which had their origins in Roman and Germanic law. The imposition of these institutions by the Japanese and their use for repressive colonial purposes constituted a sharp break from premodern Korean formal law, obliterated normal legal evolutionary processes, and produced a revolutionary impact on Korean life. Second, although the legal institutions imposed by the Japanese have been retained, the liberal orientation and content adopted following the end of World War II marks a drastic change from the repressive practices under the Japanese rule.

The pervasive influence of Western legal institutions in modern Korean history highlights the importance of studying German law as well as Roman law and its legacy. Most Korean legal scholars today focus on German and Roman law; only a few statutory provisions, mainly in family and criminal law, have their origins in traditional Korean law. However, this does not resolve the question of devising an adequate theoretical scheme for understanding the "legal revolution" described above in terms other than political upheaval–that is, the problem of the continuity of Korean legal history still remains.

Further, Western legal anthropologists in studying the customary law of primitive societies encounter legal precepts and institutions that resemble those of advanced Western law. The scholars thereby conclude that legal customs are more or less similar everywhere.[1] Such apparent

[1]Laura Nader, "Introduction" in Laura Nader, ed., *Law in Culture and Society* (Chicago: Aldine, 1969), pp. 1–10.

similarities exist also between the traditional and modern Korean legal systems. These similarities, however, obscure the more fundamental differences in the values that support the two systems. This element of bias effectively hinders a fuller understanding of the complexities of how unique legal institutions and practices operate within their own cultural settings.

Finally, not all Western legal institutions have been equally well received by traditional Korean society. Some transplanted institutions can be regarded as successes, others as failures, and still others as neither. Hence the question arises whether the successfully introduced institutions were not simply those that replaced traditional institutions performing the same functions; and whether failures are confirmations of the fact that the mere introduction of a new institution does not create changes necessary for its functioning; further, whether the failures were caused by the persistent practice of the supposedly replaced traditional institutions.

Law has many faces: retributory, punitive, compensatory, regulatory, correctional, educative; besides, there is substantive and procedural law. Law can concern a single case, it can be statutory law, it can be an institution, and it can be a whole system on varying levels of abstraction from its impact on an individual to that on a whole system. In this study, we will speak of law in terms of a whole legal system.

LAW AND LEGAL INSTITUTIONS IN TRADITIONAL KOREA

We will try to characterize traditional Korean society under the Yi dynasty (1392–1910), for the purpose of studying the history of law during the dynastic period.

The Yi period is characterized by centralized bureaucratic political organization,[2] Confucianism[3] as the official ideology, religion, a philo-

[2] The Yi dynasty's political system should be classified as "empire" according to S. N. Eisenstadt's *The Political Systems of Empires* (New York: Free Press, 1969).

[3] For the history of Confucianism in Korea, see Hyŏn Sang-yun, *Chosŏn yuhaksa* [A Korean History of Confucianism] (Seoul: Minjungsŏgwan, 1954); Sŏng Nak-hun, "Han'guk Yuhaksa" [Korean Confucian History], and "Han'guk yugyo sasangsa" [History of Korean Confucian Thought], both in *Han'guk munhwasa taegye* [Korean Cultural History Series] (Seoul: Korea University Research Institute of Korean Culture, 1970), VI, 365–447 and 909–958.

For Confucianism in China, see Chan Wing-tsin, "Confucianism" in Vergilius T. Ferm, ed., *Religion in the Twentieth Century* (New York: Philosophical Library, 1948), H. G. Creel, *Chinese Thought: From Confucius to Mao Tse-tung* (University of Chicago Press, 1953); H. H. Dubs, "Comparison of Greek and Chinese Philosophy," *Chinese Social and Political Science Review*, 17 (1933), 307–327; Fung Yu-lan, *A History of Chinese Philosophy*, trans. by Derk Bodde (Princeton University Press, 1953); Hu Shih, "Religion and Philosophy in Chinese History" in S. H. Chen Zen, ed., *Symposium on Chinese Culture* (Shanghai: China

sophical and moral foundation of the political-legal system, and the family as the "holy community."[4] Although Korea shared the features with traditional China, the extent to which they evolved in Korea far exceeded that in China, probably because of Korea's small size and its peninsular position, open to the Asian continent only to the north. These features were the result of the success with which the Korean Confucian scholar-official class established itself as the dominant ruling class. The Confucian scholar-dominated centralized political organization gave Korea the political stability that helped the yangban class to become strategically so positioned in society that no other class armed with a non-Confucian ideology was able to challenge their power monopoly.

Geographically, Korea is so situated that it could enjoy internal serenity and peace whether China and Japan were at peace or in turmoil. With stable governments on the continent and in the Japanese islands, the Yi dynasty was able to enjoy long-lasting peace almost for its entire rule until the massive waves of the Western mercantile forces reached Korea. The peace was broken only twice, in the late sixteenth and the early seventeenth centuries, when China and Japan underwent major political changes–from the Ming to the Ching dynasties in China and from the Warring Era to the Tokugawa regime in Japan. The external peace permitted the Korean Confucian rulers to concentrate on domestic matters and particularly on the construction of an ideal Confucian political order. The Chinese Confucian model, particularly that of the Tang and Ming dynasties, was the model for Korea's political order.

Korea's scholar-officials envisioned Korea as a hierarchical society based on a class division with the official-producing class, the yangban, on top (the king at its zenith) and with the material-producing commoner class at its broad base. Besides, there was the middle class, below the yangban but above the commoners, producing lower-ranking civil and military officials and specialists manning the lower echelons of the yangban-dominated bureaucratic organization; and the outcast class, at the bottom of the societal hierarchy, below the commoners, holding jobs regarded as demeaning and degrading, such as butchers, sailors, travel-

---

Institute of Pacific Relations, 1931); Joseph M. Kitagawa, *Religions of the East* (Philadelphia: Westminster, 1968), pp. 40–98; Lin Yu-tang, *My Country and My People* (New York: John Day, 1936); Lin Yu-tang, ed. and trans., *The Wisdom of Confucius* (New York: Random House, 1943); Arthur F. Wright, ed., *Studies in Chinese Thought* (University of Chicago Press, 1953); D. S. Nivison and A. F. Wright, eds., *Confucianism in Action* (Stanford University Press, 1959); A. F. Wright and D. Twitchett, eds., *Confucian Personalities* (Stanford University Press, 1963); Chan Wing-tsit, trans. and comp., *A Source Book in Chinese Philosophy* (Princeton University Press, 1963); William Theodore De Bary, et al., eds., *Sources of Chinese Tradition*, 2 vols. (New York: Columbia University Press, 1964).

[4] Kitagawa, *op. cit.* (see note 3), *Religions of the East*, p. 29.

ing musicians, entertainers, and shamans. Thus, the official stratification went with the officially established division of labor: the yangban produced the Korean version of philosopher-king in the Confucian image for the society; the middle class supplied the lower-ranking officials; the commoners furnished the farmers, craftsmen, and merchants; and the outcast provided the marginal, lowest job holders. No serious challenge to the ruling class's power monopoly was possible. Korea's small size left little room for regionalism either in the sense of the traditional Chinese context or in the sense of Japanese feudalism.

Traditional Korea was an agricultural, sedentary society. The centralized political organization relied for its economic resources on land and its products, and on manpower by way of tax in kind (corvee) and conscription. The regime's anti-commerce policies, based on the Confucian bias against profit-making, discouraged the growth of a commercial bourgeoisie engaging in foreign trade and sea-faring adventure. Foreign trade by private persons was prohibited. Domestic trade was conducted by government-licensed, privileged merchants who monopolized dealings with the court; peddlers provided towns and villages with merchandise; craftsmen were allowed to sell their surplus product at local markets while being required to supply certain amounts of goods to the government. But all these did not lead to the emergence of a commercial class in Korea comparable to a Western business class. There were only periodic markets where farmers and craftsmen traded their products. Korea's peninsular location made such anti-commerce, isolationist policies relatively easy. Thus, Korea became a vertically and horizontally closed society. This almost absolute isolation gave the Korean Confucian rulers an advantage over, for example, the Chinese rulers, in monopolizing power and practicing Confucian teachings. At the same time, however, the same isolation enabled foreign powers to take Korea simply by toppling the top of the society.

The centralization in political organization after the Chinese model, then, was stricter in Korea than in China; the Confucian ruler had a better chance to realize Confucian ideals than the Chinese rulers. Since power, wealth, and honor were all concentrated in the hands of the Confucian scholar-officials, virtually all personal goals for achievement centered on the official position in and around the government.

The essence of politics for the scholar-officials was the realization of Confucian ideals in society. The natural agency to practice ideal politics and to realize the construction of the ideal society was hard learning and self-cultivation. Through exemplary conduct in politics and private life all people were to practice Confucian teachings so that the entire society would be transformed into ideal Confucian images like those presumed as having prevailed during the pre-Yi, mythical Yao-Shun period of China.

In Confucian teachings, the family is of central importance. Confucianism may be defined as a philosophical, moral, and ethical system of thoughts on nature, society, and human beings, which does not contain a notion of God. Confucianism is secular, and it has been in fact antireligious, especially opposed to Buddhism in Korea.[5] It performed, however, some religious functions, too. Filial duty, ancestor worship, and ceremonies for Confucian sages were conducted with religious piety and enthusiasm. Basic human relations, such as father-son, prince-minister, and teacher-student, took on sacred and pious connotations. For scholar-officials, Confucianism took the place of religion, and the family was the "holy community." The family was regarded as the social foundation of law and political organization. The family, not the individual, was the basic unit (e.g., family communal property).

The political community was symbolized by the king, as the parent of the people—conceived as extended family—so that there was no qualitative difference between familial and political-legal norms: a human being had to be loyal to his king and filial to his parents; according to an old saying, a loyal minister comes from a family that produced filial sons; the normative image of the family was understood as the normative image of the state symbolized by the king, and thus norms governing family relations were the model of norms governing relationships between the monarch and his ministers, the king and his people, and the magistrate and the subject. In other words, familial norms were applied to the political dimension. Besides, the norms governing family relations were also the model for other human relations, such as those between teacher and student.

Although much less articulated ideologically, village communities also played an important role as administrative and social units. Under the parental guardianship of the magistrate, representing the patriarchal king, communal harmony was analogous with family harmony. Ideally the Confucian scholar-magistrate and the resident yangban forming the upper stratum of a locality set examples in governing and in everyday conduct for the rest of the local population. Several local organizations, such as the *hyangyak* organization[6] attempted to inculcate Confucian teachings in the local population.

---

[5] Kim Yong-tae, "Han'guk pulgyosa" [History of Korean Buddhism], in *Han'guk munhwasa taegye, op. cit.* (see note 3) VI, 269–364; *Han'guksa* [History of Korea] (Seoul: Chindan hakhoe, 1962), III, 707 ff.; Yi Sang-baek, *Han'guk munhwasa yŏn'gu non'go* [Studies on Korean Cultural History] (Seoul: Ŭryumunhwasa, 1948), pp. 1–170; Kim Dŭk-hwang, *Han'guk chongyosa* [History of Religions in Korea] (Seoul: Haemunsa, 1963), parts 3 and 4.

[6] For *Hyangyak* organization, see Pak Dŏk-pae, "Hyangyagŭi pŏpchŏk yŏn'gu" [A Study of Legal Aspects of Hyangyak Organization], *Pŏpsahak yŏn'gu* [Study of Legal History], III, 27–74 (1976); Kim Yu-hyŏk, "Hyangyagŭi yuhyŏngjŏk

Chinese influence in the form of the Confucian arts of government and of the Confucian literati tradition antedated the Yi dynasty. This influence was manifested in governmental organization, especially by the royal examinations and the emergence of Confucian scholar-officials. The Chinese Confucian classics and their neo-Confucian exegeses had to be mastered by aspiring scholar-officials; the classics were the basis for the training of rulers and literati. Confucianism was practically the sole intellectual and philosophical discipline, and creative Korean Confucian scholars contributed to it.

Confucianism is to traditional law what natural law, individual freedom, equality, the market system, liberalism, democratic revolution, and market economy, all combined, are to modern Western law. The classic expression of Confucius' thought on politics and law was: "Lead the people with governmental measures and regulate them by law and punishment, and they will avoid wrong-doing but will have no sense of honor and shame. Lead them with virtue and regulate them by rule of propriety [*ye* in Korean and *li* in Chinese], and they will have a sense of shame and, moreover, set themselves right."[7] These precepts dominated politics, morality, and law. The eighteenth-century Korean Confucian scholar Chŏng Yag-yong echoed these ideas in his *Mongmin-simsŏ*.[8] The law thus understood was equated with the command of the sovereign and, particularly, with criminal punishment.[9] The arts of politics consisted

koch'al" [A Study of the Patterns of Hyangyak Organization], *Pŏpsahak yŏn'gu*, III, 75–111; Yu Hong-yŏl, "Chosŏn hyangyagŭi sŏngnip" [On the Emergence of Korean Hyangyak Organization], Chindanhakpo, IX, 86–144 (1938); Kim Tu-hŏn, *Han'guk Kajokchedo yŏn'gu* [A Study of Korean Family System] (Seoul: Seoul National University Press, 1969), pp. 125 ff.; Tabana Tameo, *Chōsen Kyōyaku kyoka shi no kenkyū* [A Study of Korean Hyangyak and Indoctrination History] (Tokyo: Meihosah, 1972).

7 From the "Analects" in *A Source Book in Chinese Philosophy*, p. 22 (see note 3).

8 *Kugyŏk Mongminsimsŏ* [a contemporary translation of Mongminsimsŏ] (Seoul: Minjokmunhwach'ujinhoe, 1969), *passim*.

9 For the Oriental, especially the Chinese, concept of law, see Derk Bodde, "Basic Concepts of Chinese Law: The Genesis and Evolution of Legal Thought in Traditional China," in *Proceedings of the American Philosophical Society*, 107:5 (October, 1963), 375–398; Bodde and Morris, *Law in Imperial China* (University of Pennsylvania Press, 1967); Ch'u, T'ung-tsu, *Law and Society in Traditional China* (Paris: Mouton, 1961); H. G. Creel, "The Fa-chia: 'Legalists' or Administrator?" *Bulletin of the Institute of History and Philosophy*, special volume of *Academia Sinica*, IV, 607–636 (1961); H. McAleavy, "Chinese Law," in J. D. M. Derret, ed., *An Introduction to Legal Systems* (New York: Praeger, 1968), pp. 105–130; Joseph Needham, "Human Law and the Laws of Nature in China and the West," in *Science and Civilization in China*, II: *History of Scientific Thought* (Cambridge University Press, 1956), 518–583; Benjamin Schwartz, "On Attitudes Toward Law in China" in *Government Under Law and the Individual* (Washington,

in the practice of virtue and moral propriety. Therefore law in its close associations with shame and moral impropriety was conceived as destined to wither away when morality was fully realized with ideal politics. Law comes into play only when morality fails.[10] Here the Oriental notion of law departs from that of Western law.

Despite Western legal-positivist notions of law, like those of John Austin, which have no moral implications, since the time of the Greek philosophers law in the West has been regarded as associated with justice. At least the law is a moral minimum both in the sense that it is the minimum of what is required by morality and that what the law says is not morally wrong but right at the minimum. The Western notion of law is associated with what is morally right, whereas in traditional Korea law is not positively associated with what is morally right, but is something to be avoided—something the government must reserve as the last resort against a morally intractable person. The notion of law in Korea is closely associated with Oriental shame culture.[11] Law represents punishment inflicted upon one who does not know what is shameful. Law is regarded as shameful even if one follows what it says, because law tells you what to do, whereas you are expected to do what is morally right without any law telling you to do so; you are expected to be morally above the law. This notion of law still persists as part of current Korean legal culture.

Law in traditional Korea was concerned less with private relations (which form the major ingredient of English common law, Roman law, and civil law) than with the law of command and of criminal punishment. Private law was not of major legal concern as in the West, because of the towering presence of government and of Confucianism as political ideology. In modern terminology, the law was primarily concerned with "the public sector."

The kings in traditional Korea launched an energetic drive to have the basic principles and rules of law for governance codified after the Chinese models, the codes of the Ming dynasty (1368–1644), the *Minglü*. Thus there emerged the *Great Codes of Governance*, the *Kyŏngguktaejŏn* of 1471, which were designed to be the ideal code of immortality. The *Great Codes* formed the backbone of Korean political, social, legal, and

---

D.C.: American Council of Learned Societies Devoted to Humanistic Studies, 1957), pp. 27–39; Noboru Niida, *Chūgoku hōseishi* [Chinese Legal History] (Tokyo: Iwanami, 1963).

[10] Chŏng Yag-yong *Kugyŏk Mongminsimsŏ*, II, 451 ff.

[11] Shame culture is usually presented as a characteristic of Oriental culture in contrast to guilt culture in the West. Ruth Benedict, *The Chrysanthemum and the Sword* (Boston: Houghton, 1946). See also John Finley Scott, *Internalization of Norms* (Englewood Cliffs: Prentice-Hall, 1971). Scott refutes the dichotomy.

economic life, up to the time when Westernized legal codes at the turn of the century superseded them.

In establishing the *Great Codes*, the kings demonstrated that they wished to *observe* the ancient law but not to *enact* it.[12] They claimed they were adhering to the law of the blissful, idealized past, partly indigenous and partly Confucian, presumed to have prevailed in the romanticized past of the Confucian sages.

Although, then, the validity of the *Great Codes* rested on ancient law, it also rested on the infallible authority of the patriarchal king. The *Codes* were the legal manifestation of the *imperium* in the Weberian sense. Webster's dictionary has two entries defining imperium as a legal term: "right to command" and "right of jurisdiction, which includes the right to employ the force of the state to enforce the laws," indicating two aspects of law: command and sanction. Weber[13] used the word *imperium* to describe the state of law in a society in which the concept of public criminal law was established by patriarchal kings just emerging from a blood-feud society. Weber also used the word to describe, in private law, the nature of equity vis-à-vis the English common law, and *ius honorarium* vis-à-vis *ius civile* in Roman law.

Law as exercise of *imperium* was predicated by the centralized bureaucratic political system. This is not the place to discuss the controversy in the ancient period between the Confucians and the Legalists who advocated the use of legal means (i.e., punishment) rather than morality or virtue in governing the state.[14] But we note that the Legalists more than the Confucians laid the foundations of the Ch'in dynasty (third century B.C.), the first centralized bureaucratic empire in China, by advocating the command of the sovereign as the primary source of law. The subsequent dynasties owed their imperial political orders and codes to the Legalists, even though the Legalist school had long died, and Confucian thoughts dominated the Chinese intellectual world. Thus, the practical utility of the law made it an indispensable part of the centralized government. The predominant Confucian thoughts, however, were massively incorporated into the law, marking "Legalist triumph but Confucianization of law."[15]

---

[12] Preface to *Kyŏngguktaejŏn* [The Great Codes of Governance], a modern Korean translation (Seoul: Bopjaech'o, 1972) I, 1-2.

[13] Max Weber, *Economy and Society*, ed. by Guenther Roth and Claus Wittich (New York: Bedminster Press, 1968), II, 651 and 839 ff.

[14] For the Legalists, see note 9; Needham, "The Fa Chia," *Science and Civilization in China*, II, 204-215; Chan, *A Source Book in Chinese Philosophy*, pp. 251 ff.; *Sources of Chinese Tradition*, I, 122-144.

[15] Derk Bodde, "Basic Concepts of Chinese Law," *Proceedings of the American Philosophical Society*, 107:5 (October, 1963), 386.

Criminal or private law, as manifestations of the *imperium*, consist of (a) the provisions of duties and obligations of the king's officials and (b) the provisions of disciplinary measures directed at the king's officials; and of criminal punishment directed primarily at officials (judges) and secondarily at subjects at large. Such laws, therefore, are composed of provisions with the norm structure: "Do this or do not do that; otherwise you are subject to disciplinary or criminal punishment." Even when exercised in the private law field, law as manifestation of the *imperium* consists basically of the king's instructions to his officials who sit as judges. These instructions tell judges how to adjudicate private litigations. But the instructions do not directly deal with private legal relationships between parties. Private legal relationships, private rights and duties, and private rights and wrongs, can be recognized only as reflections of the legal provisions of a judicial nature, which are manifestations of the *imperium*.

The judge in a criminal trial was required to specify the legal ground for a criminal sentence.[16] Therefore, a defendant may have had the same protection as the modern doctrine of *nullum crimen, nulla poena, sine lege* would provide. The purpose of the requirement, however, was more to prevent an adjudicating official's arbitrary lawless decision than to provide protection as a right to the defendant. Thus, an adjudicating official was subject to disciplinary or criminal punishment when he failed to follow the requirement.[17] In this way the wrong done could be corrected, but not as a defendant's right; he only could file a petition for redress to the king, acceptance of which depended on the grace granted by the king.[18]

The relationships between the king and his subjects and between

[16] *Kugyŏk Taemyŏngyul Chikhae*, a modern Korean translation of *Taemyŏngyul chikhae*, the *Minglü* (the Ming Codes) in use during the Yi dynasty (Seoul: Pŏpchech'ŏ, 1964), pp. 512–513 (the rule of Tanjoeinyullyŏng: the rule for specification of the provision in point when delivering a verdict and sentence); Sŏ Il-gyo, *Chosŏn wangjo hyŏngsajedoŭi yŏn'gu* [A Study of the Criminal System of the Yi Dynasty] (Seoul : Han'guk pŏmnyŏng p'yŏnch'anhoe, 1968), pp. 81–83.

[17] See note 16. According to the rule of Tanjoeinyullyŏng of the *Minglü*, one who does not follow the rule is subject to the punishment of thirty strokes.

[18] Note, for example, *Imjarok*, a memoir written by Yu Chin, a son of the wartime prime minister during the Korean-Japanese war of Imjin (1592–1598). Yu Chin was implicated in a treason trial whose final stage was held before the king. He was acquitted. In announcing the judgment, the king stated: "Since you are a son of the late prime minister Yu who performed excellent services for the late king, I felt I could not punish you, so that the spirit of your dead father could be appeased. Thus, I decided to favor you with leniency." Yu Chin confessed in his memoirs that he almost incurred the king's anger by forgetting to thank him because of his own confusion and gratefulness. He himself was a Confucian scholar who passed the first of the royal examinations. *Wŏlgan Chungang* (*Monthly Chungang*), November 1973, pp. 163–170 and December 1973, pp. 252–261 (trans. by Hong Chae-gŏl).

parents and children, represented by loyalty and filial duty, were moral, personal relationships backed by law; they were not legal relationships. The duty of the king's officials to observe the law was intertwined with the personal relationships between the king and his ministers characterized by loyalty. According to Chŏng Yag-yong: "The law is an order of the king. Therefore, one who does not follow the law is like one who does not obey an order of his king."[19] An order of the king is a manifestation of the *imperium.*

The *Great Codes* consisted of six codes: *Ijŏn, Hojŏn, Yejŏn, Pyŏngjŏn, Hyŏngjŏn,* and *Kongjŏn. Ijŏn* included provisions for bureaucratic organization, hierarchies for civil officials, and their appointment and dismissal. *Hojŏn's* provisions covered household census and registration, land tenure, and taxes. *Yejŏn* was concerned with rituals and ceremonies, education, and the royal examination for recruitment of civil officials. *Pyŏngjŏn* had provisions for military organization and military bureaucratic hierarchies, for the royal examination for recruitment of military officials and for military services. *Hyŏngjŏn* provided for criminal law and procedures, and the servant (slave) system. Finally, *Kongjŏn* regulated official constructions and civil engineering, and official artisans and craftsmen. The provisions of the *Great Codes* were predominantly for governmental organization, offices, the scholar-official bureaucracy, governmental business, behavioral standards for officials, and criminal law. In their structure, they were manifestations of the *imperium.* Consequently, they were provisions of duties and obligations addressed to the king's officials. Only criminal provisions were addressed also to the subjects at large and secondarily.

There were no provisions for legal rights; the *Great Codes* were composed of provisions of duties and obligations alone. Any norm, including a legal norm, is either a duty or an obligation, according to Hans Kelsen.[20] The notion of right is a modern Western invention primarily influenced by the Enlightenment and natural law.[21] Besides, in Roman law and English law substantive rights evolved from *actio* or action, a procedural right to sue in court. In traditional Korea, rightful interests were legally and judicially protected not because they were legal rights but because they were actionable rights. Moreover, the Confucian political ideology left no room for legal rights and confined itself to philosophical, moral, and behavioral notions of justice and of what is right and wrong. The two essential elements of the Confucian normative system, loyalty to the king and filial duty, defy quantification. Ideologically, a set limit or

[19] Chŏng Yag-yong, *Kugyŏk Mongminsimsŏ,* I, 167.

[20] Hans Kelsen, *The Pure Theory of Law,* trans. by Max Knight (1970), pp. 114 ff.

[21] See Roscoe Pound, *Jurisprudence* (St. Paul: West Publishing Co., 1959), IV, 41 ff.

amount, which goes usually with modern legal rights and duties, is incompatible with the Confucian normative system. The traditional Korean legal system, then, was not built on the modern notions of legal rights reciprocated by legal duties.

As mentioned, most provisions of the *Great Codes* were in public law, dealing with power relations. In traditional Korea, public law did not arise from private relations; private law did not emerge as a distinctive set of legal rules separated from the area of public relations. Even in adjudication, for instance, private matters, which concerned only private parties, were regarded as having minor importance, compared with matters of public concern; they were given low priority or dispensed with altogether. Thus, the aspects of private law that in the West worked in the form of property rights and freedom of contract as legal restraints placed on the exercise of power, are missing from the provisions of the *Great Codes*. To be sure, the codes had provisions closely related to matters which could be private in modern terms, for instance those of land tenure, slave ownership, and adjudication of law suits between private parties. Their legal structure, however, consisted also in the exercise of the *imperium*. For example, a private suit was prohibited after the statute of limitation passed (five years in the *Great Codes* but later extended to thirty years). A person who filed a suit after the statute of limitation passed, and also the official who processed it, was subject to punishment.[22] The substantive rules of possible private interests were provided because of their importance for the political-legal order of society. The adjudicatory rules were adopted because adjudication of private litigations was important government business despite the Confucian ideological bias against disputes and litigations. Differentiation between a private and a public sphere of life is incompatible with the Confucian ideology.

The private spheres of life, which were not covered by the provisions of the *Great Codes*, were left to customary law and judicial precedents. Only a small part of the vast body of customary law and judicial precedents developed during the Yi dynasty has been systematically studied by modern scholars.[23] In traditional Korea, there was no jurisprudence as an

---

[22] Pak Pyŏng-ho, *Han'guk pŏpchesago* [A Study of Korean Legal History] (Seoul: Pomunsa, 1974), pp. 261–267.

[23] See Pak Pyŏng-ho, "Yijosidaeŭi pudongsansosongbop sogo" [A Study of the Court Procedure for Immovable Property Litigation During the Yi dynasty], *Seoul Law Journal*, 2:1 (1960), 27–66; *Han'guk pŏpchesa t'ŭsuyŏn'gu: Yijosidaeŭi pudongsanmaemae gŭp tambobŏp* [A Study of the Legal History of Korea: Laws of Sales and Security of Immovable Property in the Yi Dynasty], Korean Research Center, Korean Studies Series, IV (1960); "Hyojong inyŏnŭi hansŏngbu *kyŏlsong iban*" [Seoul City Government Decision Rendered in 1661], *Hyangt'o Seoul*, 17 (1963), 117–137; "Han'guk kŭnseŭi t'ojisoyugwŏne kwanhan yŏn'gu" [A Study of

autonomous intellectual discipline concerned with the study of customary law, judicial precedents, or the provisions of the *Great Codes* either for intellectual inquiry or for the practical needs of legislation, adjudication, and legal practice. Confucian ideology was too dominant to leave room for a jurisprudence. In their generalist Confucian outlook the scholar-officials refused to be experts in practical matters like law. Therefore, there were no jurisprudential treatises, law books, or intellectually inspired compilations of law other than the *Great Codes* and their subsequent codes, officially compiled precedents, judicial records, and law-related practical guidance books like the *Muwŏllok*, a medical-legal handbook. To know today what law was in the private sphere of life, one has to look into the untapped old official and private documents, records, letters, and diaries, including judicial records, all written in Chinese characters. The difficulty of such a pioneering study and the lack of practical utility do not inspire modern legal scholars to undertake such a study.

Lack of differentiation—or lack of autonomy of law from morality and politics—is most striking in the governmental structure related to justice administration. The generalist scholar-officials were appointed as magistrates, governors, ministers (including the minister of justice), and other officials. For instance, the magistrate, who alone was in charge of the central government's business (including taxes, police, and even military matters in his district), functioned as judge at the same time. Structural differentiation between adjudicative, legislative, and administrative business was regarded as an obstacle to realizing Confucian substantive justice. Substantive justice can be attained more easily with less structural differentiation. The adjudicatory function was practically an extension of the administrative function of the patriarchal king.[24] Structural differentiation was attained to some extent at the level of legal-judicial assistants for the magistrate judge, and for the provincial governors, and at the low echelon of some ministries like the Minister of Justice. However, the social esteem and power of those assistants were inferior to those of the yangban official.

Jurisdictions for legally-judicially related ministerial offices, including the Ministry of Justice, at the king's court were not well defined; they overlapped in many cases.[25] Civil adjudication was not clearly demarcated from criminal trial; in criminal trials, there was no clear-cut distinction

---

Land-ownership in Premodern Korea], *Seoul Law Journal*, 8:1 (1966), 63–97 and 78–106; *Chŏnt'ongjŏk pŏpch'egyewa pŏbŭisik* [Traditional Legal System and Attitude], 1972; and *Han'guk pŏpchesago* (1974), *op. cit.* (see note 22).

[24] See Sŏ Il-gyo, *Chosŏn wangjo hyŏngsajedoŭi yŏn'gu*, *op. cit.* (see note 19), pp. 7 ff. and p. 414 (see note 16).

[25] *Ibid.*, pp. 7–15.

between the pre-indictment investigatory stage and the post-indictment trial stage, and between police investigation, prosecution, and trial.[26] At a local level, the magistrate performed all functions of the investigation, indictment, trial, and implementation of judgment in a criminal case.

Positive law of the Yi dynasty was characterized by its substantive rationality outweighing its formal rationality in Weberian analytic terms.[27] As indicated earlier, administration of justice was an extension of the government's administrative function. In judicial function, virtually every kind of adjudication was criminal trial in the sense that any adjudication could result in criminal punishment.[28] A civil suit, for example, may have involved one who took all the family fortune in inheritance without sharing it with other rightful heirs, one who illegally seized another's land or house, or one who failed to pay debts. In such suits, judgment on the criminal elements was made in a proceeding incidental to or following the main proceeding of the litigation, even though there was no formally instituted criminal charge in the initial complaint filed at the court.[29] Thus, it was common that a party filed a civil complaint as well as a criminal charge at the same time against the same defendant.[30] It was provided that in a civil suit arising from a dispute between brothers or relatives, trial took place after criminal punishment.[31] A civil case was not even heard during

[26] *Ibid.*, pp. 263–432.

[27] C. K. Yang talks about "formal rule" as one of the characteristics of Chinese bureaucracy. See his "Some Characteristics of Chinese Bureaucratic Behavior," in Nivison and Wright, eds., *Confucianism in Action*, *op. cit.* (see note 3) pp. 134–164. Yang says: "A system of formal rules was a well-developed feature of the Chinese bureaucracy." His "formalism" in traditional China seems to be somewhat misleading, because he starts his discussion on Chinese formal rules of law by citing Weberian concepts. Certainly, bureaucracy goes with a degree of formal quality, without which a bureaucracy cannot function. This was also true in China and Korea. Besides, in terms of substantive justice and in terms of codification of substantive rules, it may well be that medieval Oriental formal law was more developed than that of the contemporary Western societies and even as much as that of the present-day Western societies, if the differences between the Orient and the West in the values and cultural premises underlying their "formal law" are understood.

In our opinion, however, the Oriental formal legal rules lacked the formal quality of Western law. The formal rationality in Western law can be represented by the presence of a group of legal professionals structurally and functionally separated from and independent of the members of the ruling elites of society, and by the development of jurisprudence as an autonomous discipline separated from the rest of society's cherished intellectual tradition and learning.

[28] Pak Pyŏng-ho, *Han'guk pŏpchesago*, *op. cit.* (see note 22), pp. 261–267.

[29] Ibid., pp. 251–252.

[30] Ibid., pp. 251–252.

[31] See the Provision of *Ch'ŏngri* (Hearing) in *Soktaejŏn* (The Subsequent Great

the busy agricultural season lasting from the vernal to the autumnal equinox[32] because it was not considered serious enough unless it had a criminal aspect. It was provided further that no complaint requesting payment of debts be even heard in a lean year,[33] obviously because of Confucian humanism.

An example of substantive rationality outweighing formal rationality is analogy allowed in criminal trial.[34] On each occasion, however, the judge was required to have the king's permission to apply analogy. Otherwise, formal legal ground was required for each criminal sentence in terms of a formal legal provision. The prevailing notion of law was that debts must be judicially forgiven, criminal sentences reduced, and a criminal defendant acquitted when sufficiently mitigating circumstances existed in terms of substantive justice.[35] Confucian moral standards formed the contents of substantive justice.

Scholar-officials required to execute the law had to follow their moral dictates rather than rules.[36] An official sticking to the letter of the law was considered "a little man." Further, it was believed that once one attained by self-cultivation and hard work the moral and intellectual achievement of a philosopher-king or the *to* of a *kunja* (in Chinese *tao* of a *kuntzu*, the Way of a superior man), one had already left the mundane world of rules and regulations. Ideally, the rulers of the Yi dynasty were supposed to have attained that level of moral and intellectual achievement. In other words, the political-legal system of the Yi dynasty was built on the image of the ideal ruler. Without him there was no way to guarantee substantive justice because substantive rationality (substantive justice) outweighed formal rationality. Confucianism was reserved for the

---

Codes in modern Korean translation, Seoul: Pŏpchech'ŏ, 1965), p. 316; Pak Pyŏng-ho, *Han'guk pŏpchesago*, pp. 260–261; Chŏng Yag-yong, *Kugyŏk Mongminsimsŏ*, II, 374 ff.; *Wŏnsinbo Sugyŏ'imnok-Sasŏngnyuch'wi* (New Enlarged Edition of Compilation of the King's Instructions–Adjudicatory Precedents in modern Korean translation, published in Seoul: Pŏpchech'ŏ, 1964), p. 140 [No. 657, the Provision of Kŭmje: (Interdictions)].

[32] See the Provision of Chŏngsong (Stay of Hearing) in *Kyŏngguktaejŏn*, II, 174; Pak Pyŏng-ho, *Han'guk pŏpchesago*, p. 267.

[33] See the Provisions of Chŏngsong (State of Hearing) in *Soktaejŏn*, p. 295; Pak Pyŏng-ho, *Han'guk pŏpchesago*, p. 268.

[34] See the Provision of Tanjoemujŏngjo (Decision in Absence of the Right Provision) in *Taemyŏngyulchikhae*, *op. cit.* (n. 16), pp. 99–100; Sŏ Il-gyo, *Chosŏn wangjohyŏngsajedoŭi yŏn'gu*, *op. cit.* (n. 16), pp. 81–83.

[35] *Wŏnsinbo Sugyojiprok-Sasŏngnyuch'wi*, *op. cit.* (n. 31), p. 419 (No. 1240); Chŏng Yag-yong, *Kugyŏk Mongminsimsŏ*, II, 402 ff. and 407 ff.

[36] See King Yŏngjo's preface to the *Soktaejŏn*, *op. cit.* (n. 31). He advises to follow the dictate (*taeŭi*) rather than the details (*sejŏl*) of the provisions.

rulers. The ruled belonged to the mundane world of the law. Confucian teachings were not required for the ruled even to learn. On the other hand, the rulers were placed above the law.

Why did substantive rationality outweigh formal rationality in the traditional Korean system? Why was there no such formal rationality as that in the English common law? For example there were forms for filing complaints but there was no notion of *action* in the English law.[37] There was a rule as a manifestation of the *imperium* providing that no one was allowed to relitigate following three successful proceedings at the courts of different levels,[38] but there was no notion of *collateral estoppel* or *res judicata*. As we have seen, there was no jurisprudence as an intellectual discipline of systematic knowledge of law and legal system except for a body of practical knowledge of law as a skill, called *YurHak*, which the scholar-officials to whom the law was entrusted for its administration disdained and which thus had to be learned by "middle men." Why? It seems that the answer lies in the nature of the bureaucracy of the Yi dynasty, which was to administer the law, on the one hand, and in Confucian teachings, which provided to the ruling yangban, including those appointed as officials, the system of behavioral norms and the frameworks of learning and personality needed for the rulers.

In England the administration of law depended on the monopolist hands of the bar, which was formed by gradually excluding the clergyman from the field of law. Professional training was entirely placed at the hands of the bar. The judges, especially, were recruited from the members of the bar. Lawyers were primarily interested in solving for their clients routine legal matters like contracts and litigations. Following judicial precedents actually served their monetary interests. Newly enacted statutes also depended for their interpretation on the judges who were thus trained.[39] On the European Continent, however, the universities were in charge of legal education. Only those trained in jurisprudence as an autonomous intellectual discipline of systematic knowledge of law were recruited as judges, public prosecutors, and practicing lawyers after they passed a bar examination and served an internship. Hence it was natural that legal concepts, having emerged in systematic study of law at a university, were abstract legal norms derived by formal logic.[40]

In traditional Korea, however, the yangban scholar-officials were recruited through royal examinations in which successful competition

[37] See Pak Pyŏng-ho, *Han'guk pŏpchesago*, *op. cit.*, (n. 22), pp. 258 ff.

[38] Ibid., pp. 286–287.

[39] Weber, *Economy and Society*, II, 785 ff.

[40] Ibid., pp. 789 ff.

depended on the candidates' mastery of Confucian classics. Success in the examination required long hard work starting from the candidate's early childhood with the beginner's course, *Ch'ŏnjamun* (the Thousand Character Text), and going beyond his adolescence to his adulthood, sometimes up to his thirties and forties, and requiring the full command of the Confucian classics, *Sasŏsamgyŏng* (the *Four Books* and the *Three Classics*). In the examination, the *Great Codes* were test topics.[41] The scholar-officials, especially those appointed as magistrates, were required to have also a practical knowledge of the law. Of course there were thinkers such as Chŏng Yag-yong who in his *Mongminsimsŏ* deplored the fact that local magistrates loved writing poems and literary prose while neglecting legal studies.[42] For these magistrates, learning consisted mainly in studying Confucian and Chinese classics. They were moralists, philosophers, and literature writers; they were generalists and disliked to be experts in practical matters (such as law).

There was, however, a group of professionals specialized in law. And there was a special institution designed to train them and examine them.[43] They were, however, recruited from the ranks of "middle men" whose social status and power were below that of the yangbans. They acted as legal assistants and help for the yangban officials. They never developed into a professional group pursuing their own interests separate from those of the yangbans. They never developed an autonomous world outlook different from that of the scholar-officials.

There was "a group of individuals who as a means of living roamed around the magistrate courts to instigate or entice others to conduct litigation."[44] Private parties ignorant of the court procedures relied for practical help on those individuals versed in court and litigation matters.

[41] *Kyŏngguktaejŏn, op. cit.* (n. 12), I, 204, and II, 63. The *Kyŏngguktaejŏn*, along with *Karye* (Family Codes of Etiquette and Rituals, originating from Chu Tzu's family codes of etiquette and rituals) was provided as one of the required test topics for the second-stage test of the royal examination for civil officials. As for the second-stage test for military officers, the *Kyŏngguktaejŏn* was also a required test topic, but the *Karye* was not required.

[42] Chŏng Yag-yong, *Kugyŏk Mongminsimsŏ*, II, 430.

[43] According to the provisions of the *Kyŏngguktaejŏn* dealing with the royal examinations for recruitment of specialist officials other than the two major groups of Yangban officials (civil and military officers) *Taemyŏngyul* (the *Minglu*), *Tangyulsoŭi* (the Tanglüshui, an exegesis on Tanglu), *Muwŏnllok* (Wuyuanlu, a medical-legal handbook), *Yurhakhaeŭi* (Luhsuechiaii, an exegesis on Minglu), *Yurhakp'yŏnŭi* (Luhsue pieni, an exegesis on Minglu), and the *Kyŏnguk'taejŏn* were the required test topics for the royal examination for legal specialists (*yulgwa*).

[44] Pak Pyŏng-ho, *Chŏnt'ongjŏk pŏpch'egyewa pŏbŭisik, op. cit.* (n. 23), pp. 37–38; *Han'guk pŏpchesago, op. cit.* (n. 22), pp. 315 ff.

The latter wrote complaints for their clients, advised them in litigation strategy, or appeared before the court to proceed on their clients' behalf. They were compensated for their service if they won. In their function, they were similar to modern lawyers or at least to judicial scriveners. Their legitimate place in society, however, was never recognized by the yangban officials. The yangban considered them robbers who fostered litigious attitudes, caused delays,[45] and thus harmed the Confucian ideals of virtuous politics, good morals, and social harmony. The yangban prevented the emergence of an autonomous legal system and jurisprudence.

Here we need to take another look at Confucianism, particularly the neo-Confucianism of the twelfth century in China. Substantive rationality in the Yi dynasty resulted partly from the absence of a group of legal professionals differentiated from the yangbans, and partly from the nature of Confucianism, which was the ideological basis of the yangban bureaucratic organization. The essence of Confucian government was the reconstruction of an ideal society like that of the Yao and Shun period and the realization of the teachings of Confucius and Confucian sages in contemporary society. The teaching can be epitomized in the Confucian precept for politicians: "Cultivate yourself morally, control your household, and then go on to govern the country." The yangban class was expected to produce such rulers.

Since the Confucian ideal depended for its realization primarily on learning and moral achievement of individual rulers,[46] behavioral norms

---

[45] See note 46, below.

[46] Confucianism stresses moral self-cultivation more than cultivating others. When Tzu-lu asked Confucius about the superior man, Confucius said: "The superior man cultivates himself so as to give all people security and peace. To cultivate oneself so as to give all people security and peace, even Yao and Shun found it difficult to do." *Analects*, in *A Source Book in Chinese Philosophy*, pp. 43 and 605 ff.; Yi Yul-gok, *Kyŏngmong yogyŏl: Kugyŏk Yulgokchip* [Works of Yulgok], a modern Korean translation (1968), pp. 423 ff.: Chŏng Yag-yong, *Mongminsimsŏ, passim*, especially the chapter "kiyul Yukcho" [Six Rules for Controlling Oneself].

Moral self-cultivation is closely related to moral awakening, the *Way*, of the religious nirvana as the philosophical ground of the Oriental compromise in dispute settlement that Northrop calls "radical empiricism." See F. S. C. Northrop, "The Mediational Approval Theory of Law in American Legal Realism," *Virginia L. R.*, 34 (1958), 347-363; and "The Comparative Philosophy of Comparative Law," *Cornell L. Q.*, 45 (1960), 617-658. The road to reach the *Way* is up to individual endeavor. Awakening is an individual experience. Once awakening is reached, however, a person is one whole. Philosophically, the ground for mediation or compromise lies in the *Way*. Confucius said: "The superior man identifies with others but is not conciliatory." See the "Analects," in *A Source Book in Chinese Philosophy*, p. 41. Only the morally inferior man who is not awakened fights with others over a trivial matter, because he is not able to see the *Way* but only the trivial matter. Thus, occurrence of an undesirable happening or something mischievous is ascribed to moral failure or defect on the part of the

applying to rulers were Confucian moral norms, above the world of positive law. The targets of examination, review, or impeachment in the traditional governmental censoral institutions (*daegan*), which performed the functions of modern judicial review of governmental actions, and in the traditional institution of petition (*sangso*), which was the functional equivalent to modern free speech, were not so much violations of law as violations of Confucian moral norms on the part of rulers. In the political-legal system of the Yi dynasty, principles and rules that would restrain the abuse of the *imperium* were found in Confucian moral norms.

In the West, rules of restraints, designed to rationalize political power and to prevent its abuse, resulted in the liberal democratic political order. The body of such rules may be termed, for our purpose, "public law in a narrow sense." In traditional Korea, however, "man above institution" was the rule for restraint of power.

The body of "public law" (in the mentioned narrow sense) includes the following three institutional, procedural, and substantive law principles and rules: (1) Separation of power and related principles and rules, including those of checks and balances, judicial independence, rule of law, and the German principle of *Rechtsstaat*, one of whose assumptions is to maximize the freedom of the individual from government intervention. (2) Law designed in such a way as to have an action of *ultra vires* or an

---

individual (especially the ruler) rather than to its cause (natural or human), because Confucianism places its emphasis on a conciliatory attitude deriving from the achieved stage of moral self-cultivation in individuals. Therefore, the question of who is right and who is wrong in a dispute is only secondarily important.

The ruler is seen as the moral mirror of the people. When the ruler is the first to do what is morally right, people will follow his example and criminal law will not be needed. However, when the ruler is not morally right, people will not be morally right even with vigorous application of criminal law. These notions run through the pages of Chŏng Yag-yong's *Mongminsimsŏ*. (See, for example, *Kugyŏk Mongminsimsŏ*, II, 451.) They are central to the thought of Confucius. The idea that the ruler ought to be the moral model of people is emphasized here and there in the "Analects" (see *A Source Book in Chinese Philosophy*). For example (p. 41): "If a ruler sets himself right, he will be followed without his command. If he does not set himself right, even his commands will not be obeyed."

Chŏng Yag-yong, in the preface to his *Mongminsimsŏ*, asserts that half of the learning of the superior man is self-cultivation and the other half is tending the people. In the first part of the section on Ch'ŏnsong (Hearing) of the *Hyŏngjŏn Yukcho* (Six Rules of the Criminal Code) in the *Mongminsimsŏ*, he defines the Confucian moral rules applying to the judge in his adjudicatory function in the following way: "The essence of hearing a law suit lies in sincerity, and the essence of sincerity lies in watching over one's own self when alone." See *Kugyŏk Mongminsimsŏ*, II, 361. The section on *Subŏp* (Observance of Law) discusses a ruler's self-cultivation and moral rules rather than legal topics such as legal restraints placed on the ruler and legal sanctions. See *Kugyŏk Mongminsimsŏ*, I, 168 ff.

abuse of governmental power made void, not only as a legal reflection of official correction of a wrong governmental action and disciplinary or criminal punishment of a wrongdoing official at government initiative, but also as a legal right of an aggrieved private person at his initiative; besides, a wrong done by a governmental official constitutes an actionable tort on the part of the government, for which an aggrieved person can claim damage and can ask for compensation and for other remedy. (3) Damage claims, remedies, corrections of wrongs, and voidance of actions as legal rights of citizens against the government, not merely petitions or legal reflections.

Much of what is mentioned under (1) to (3) could be subsumed under the better heading of "judicial review." Moreover, although the concept of formal rationality is not identical with that of public law in our definition, they overlap. Formal rationality has also been conducive to liberal democracy in the West as interwoven with the principles of public law. The level of formal rationality in contemporary Western law was not present in traditional Korean formal law, as we have seen. Legally the level of formal rationality that obtained in the traditional Korean scene, however, was associated only with the traditional positive law as exercise of *imperium*; it was maintained by *imperium*. The principles of public law, including judicial review, were not definitely parts of traditional Korean law. In traditional Korea, the Confucian moral principals were the functional equivalents of public law. On the whole, the Confucian equivalents were successful in taming political power.

Although Confucianism has no notion of God, as we have seen, concerning the authority of the king, Confucianism performed the role of state religion in its support. All ceremonies and rites at the governmental offices and at the royal court were controlled by Confucianism. Confucianism, particularly neo-Confucianism in Korea, performing the function of medieval Catholicism in a European Inquisition heresy trial, opposed the new Confucian teaching of the *Yangming* school and subsequently the newly introduced Catholicism in the late Yi dynasty. The xenophobic anti-Western isolationist policies of the late Yi dynasty had the backing of religious Confucianism, which considered as heresy the policy of Open Door.[47] Neo-Confucianism was not readily compatible with a Western legal system whose formal rationality was biased in favor of commercial values.

---

[47] Ch'oe Ch'ang-gyu, *Han'guginŭi chŏngch'iŭisik* [*Korean Political Attitude*] (Seoul: Seoul National University Han'gungmunhwayŏn'guso, 1971); and Chong Jae-sik, "Christianity as a Heterodoxy: An Aspect of General Cultural Orientation in Traditional Korea," in *Korea's Response to the West*, ed. Yung-Hwan Jo (Kalamazoo, Mich.: The Korean Research and Publications, 1971), pp. 57–86.

David Apter's two types of traditionalism—the instrumental-hierarchical type and the consummatory-pyramidal type, as well as the former's more secular and

LAW UNDER JAPANESE RULE

For the period between the end of Korean isolation by the forcing of the Open Door and the Japanese occupation, that is, for the period between 1876 and 1910–1945, just enough facts will be presented to provide an historical perspective.

Korea came to have a civil-law legal system, specifically a German system, as a legacy of Japanese rule, but one might speculate that the same system would have been adopted even without Japanese rule. This Western system was forced on the Koreans against their interests by the Japanese, as an instrument of political and economic domination. Consequently, Koreans came to learn Western law through the examples and precedents that the Japanese set for their Korean rule. This factor has serious implications for the state of the present Western law.

Xenophobia backed by Confucianism as practiced during the isolationist period reasserted itself in the shape of nationalism after the introduction of Western reforms. The isolationist policies sound irrational but are understandable; Korea had a self-sufficient agricultural economy, which had nothing to gain by opening its doors to Western capitalism. Korea could offer only meager agricultural products as raw materials for imported machine-made goods. Once the door was open, Korea invited the competition of the world powers, whose aggression it was powerless to resist.

The door was forced open by an international treaty with Japan at Kanghwa (1876), which was brought about by the fall of the powerful regent Daewonkun and by Japan's big-gun diplomacy. But these events produced no modern reforms and introduced no Western political and social institutions. An attempt made in 1884 by a few foreign-educated reform-minded young political leaders to launch an ambitious modernization program ended up as a failure.

Reform measures, characterized by governmental introduction of Western institutions, including legal ones, started with the *Kab-o* reform (1894–1895). The first Western-style court system structurally and functionally differentiated from other functions of government was the result of the Court Organization Law of 1895, which was a part of the *Kab-o* reform.[48] The *Kab-o* reform was a series of hasty measures producing

---

military character and the latter's essentially religious and theocratic nature—can be represented respectively by Japan and Korea. "Traditionalism and Political Modernization of Ghana and Uganda," in David Apter, *Some Conceptual Approaches to the Study of Modernization* (Englewood Cliffs, N. J.: Prentice-Hall, 1968).

[48] As for the Western law and legal institutions introduced at this stage, see *Hanmal kŭndae pŏmnyŏngjaryojip* [The Source Book of Modern Laws, Orders, and Regulations of the Late Yi Dynasty] (Seoul: The National Assembly, 1970–1972),

many laws within a short period, and allowing barely enough time for Korean participants to translate into Korean the Japanese versions of these laws. Japan thus forced the Korean government to accept broad Westernization measures after the model of the Japanese Meiji Reformation (1868). Japan had a monopolist hold on Korea after the Sino-Japanese War. In Korea Westernization and loss of sovereign power proceeded at the same pace. Starting with the unequal treaty of Kangwha, Korea found her sovereign power restrained by foreign forces until her sovereignty was lost to the Japanese in 1910.

The Japanese were anxious to have the reluctant Koreans introduce unpopular Western general and legal institutions conflicting with traditions, values, and institutions. They may have been eventually introduced anyway, but the characteristic point was that the Japanese introduced them forcibly. The Decree for Haircut of 1895, *Tanballyŏng*, under which the king and the crown prince had to set an example, was symbolically important. Upon promulgation of the Decree for Haircut, nationwide armed revolts headed by Confucian scholars took place in protest.[49] In fact, it was a revolt against the Japanese. Korean attitudes toward reform legislations ranged from armed revolts to unwilling cooperation.[50]

As for the Decree for Haircut, hair was a symbol of the Confucian order, because hair was regarded as bestowed by one's parents, hence haircutting was considered "unfilial." Symbolically, therefore, the decree was designed to destroy the Confucian political order of the Yi dynasty, so that the Japanese could increase their domination over Korea. The anti-decree movement, headed by conservative Confucian scholars, allowed the Japanese to fish in troubled water and to identify whom to fight. Government armed forces were sent to local areas to quell the rebellious anti-decree "righteous forces," while Japanese garrison forces were in charge of the capital. One Confucian scholar, Ch'oe Ik-hyŏn, who headed

9 vols.; *T'onggambu pŏmnyŏng jaryojip* [The Source Book of the Laws, Orders, and Regulations of the Resident-General] (Seoul: The National Assembly, 1972–1973) 3 vols.; Kim Pyŏng-hwa, *Kŭndaehan'guk chaep'ansa* [Modern Korean Judicial History] (Seoul: Han'guk sabŏphaengjŏng hakhoe, 1974), and *Sok Kŭndaehan'guk chaep'ansa* [Supplement], 1976; *Han'guk pŏpkwansa* [A Korean History of Judges] (Seoul: The Supreme Court of Korea, 1975); Pak Pyŏng-ho, *Han'guk pŏpchesago, op. cit.* (n. 22).

[49] Ibid., VI, 701 ff.; *Tongnip undongsa* [History of the Nationalist Movement] (Seoul: Tongnip Yugongjasaŏp kigŭmunyŏng wiwŏnhoe, 1970), Vol. 1: *Ŭibyŏng hangjaengsa* [History of the Struggle of the Righteous Armies], pp. 287–428.

[50] For example, the number of the traditional educational institutions (*sŏdang*), along with the number of students attending them, sharply increased during 1912–1919 as an expression of Korean nationalism, whereas that of modern schools decreased during the same period. *Taehan'guksa* [History of Korea] (Seoul: Sint'aeyangsa, 1973), IX, 115–117.

a group of anti-decree "righteous forces," surrendered to royal Korean government forces stating that he rose to fight the Japanese, not to fight the royal army sent by his lord.[51]

Symbolic values, such as the haircut, were associated with all Western institutions, including the newly introduced legal system, albeit in varying degrees, because the destruction of five-hundred-year-old law was involved. Further involved here was not a mere reform of old institutions but their replacement by institutions violently conflicting with the old ones.

Every society has competition, conflicts, and disputes between groups and between individuals. The ideological evaluations vary, however, from society to society. In the West, competition, conflicts, and disputes have not always been perceived negatively but also positively as leading to social solidarity, progress, and other desirable changes, as attested by Simmel and Marx. In the Orient, however, they were always perceived negatively; social harmony was viewed as a paramount virtue.[52] Broken peace was equated with moral degradation, attributed to moral shortcomings of the rulers. Adam Smith's *Wealth of Nations* presents competition as leading to harmony. In the West, free competition has been assigned romantic, positive recognition and plays a role as an important social theory and practice. In the Orient, however, competition never acquired such recognition, at least as a social theory or doctrine in the Confucian intellectual tradition. No doubt, individual ability and competition played important roles in the bureaucratic and military organizations, especially in the royal examinations, but the Confucian theory stressed the ruler's obligation to take parental care of his people rather than competition. The ruler was obligated to suppress tyrannous officials, the rich, and the strong, while siding with the weak and aggrieved subjects.[53] In the Orient, a promise had to be kept. It was considered a philosophical and moral principle of correspondence between word and action (*ŏnhaeng ilch'i*) or a moral matter or a matter of "face" between neighbors or friends. But it was not recognized as an important social theory or as a legal concept as expressed in the theory of social contract and the doctrine of *pacta sunt servanda*.

The Western democratic political order and legal system, especially

---

[51] See note 49, above.

[52] Confucius said: "In hearing litigations, I am as good as anyone. What is necessary is to enable people not to have litigations at all" (*A Source Book*, p. 88).

[53] In the "Kump'ok" (Subjugation of Despots) section on the *Hyŏngjŏn yukcho* (six rules of criminal code) in his *Mongminsimsŏ*, Chŏng Yag-yong talks mainly about the problems of this Oriental protective justice, namely matters related to the problems of how to protect the weak people from the powerful and from the rich. *Kugyŏk Mongminsimsŏ*, III, 22 ff.

Western court procedures, are built on value premises of free competition and freedom of contract. Litigation and court proceedings in the West constitute a competition between private persons; the attorney system in litigation consummates competition at the court and thus contributes to the realization of justice. Therefore, denial of assistance of counsel is tantamount to denial of justice when competition is impossible, or meaningless because of great disparity between the parties in their economic power. The old Korean legal system, however, presents another picture in a lawsuit: the ideal of lawsuit and court proceedings was that the magistrate as "the parent of the people" was to suppress tyranny of low-ranking officials[54] and, further, that the magistrate allowed people with whatever grievances to come to court as they would come to their parents' home to have their grievances heard.[55] Those who, for a fee, would draw up complaint forms and conduct litigations on behalf of others—the functional equivalents of modern attorneys—were looked upon as robbers, fabricating evidence, causing delays, instigating litigations, and thus harming justice. Therefore, the reception of the Western legal system, including the attorney system, introduced alien value premises, incompatible with those of traditional Korean.

The Western law and legal system of Korea under Japanese rule (and today) shared with those of Japan proper many features of the civil-law tradition[56]: their Roman-law origin, the prominent roles played by legal scholars, universities, and legislators (rather than by judges), codified laws being the major sources of law with no rule of *stare decisis*, and an inquisitorial rather than accusatorial (or adversary) nature of court procedure. To the law and legal system of Korea under Japanese rule, however, were added particular features which made the law of Korea then distinctive even from the Japanese version of German (Western) law and legal system of Japan proper.

There was no institutional or procedural device of separation of power in the colonial government of the Japanese governor-general. He had unrestrained executive and legislative power, the latter exercised by issuing decree,[57] under the authority of the Law Concerning Laws and Orders to be Implemented in Korea, an act of the Japanese Imperial Diet.

---

[54] Chŏng Yag-yong, *Kugyŏk Mongminsimsŏ*, II, 433 ff.

[55] Ibid., II, 364.

[56] John H. Merryman, *The Civil Law Tradition* (Stanford, Calif.: Stanford University Press, 1969).

[57] See *Seirei* (the source books of the decrees of the governor-general) (Tokyo: Japanese Ministry of Foreign Affairs Bureau of Treaties, 1960 and 1961), two volumes.

There was no autonomy of the judicial department; the courts were subordinate administrative organizations of the governor-general's government.[58] There was no constitutional law in Korea, nor even a nominal or semantic constitution in Loewenstein's terms.

With no constitutional law, no separation of power, and no constitutional guarantees of human rights, there was no judicial review of the exercise of political power.[59] There was no bill of rights for Koreans. There was no notion of torts committed by the government against which a private person could claim damages. There was no way for a detained criminal defendant to request compensation from the government if he was acquitted as innocent (as provided in the present constitutional law of Korea). Koreans had nothing, as a right, to claim redress for abuse of the government-general's power, no right to be vindicated against the government at the court. The legal system of Korea under Japanese rule was a system composed essentially of rules of duties and obligations alone.

Under Japanese rule no system of positive moral norms existed applying to the rulers, designed to curb their power. There were no positive Confucian moral norms to apply to the rulers in their governing the ruled, in close association with the legal system, as in the political-legal system of the Yi dynasty. Expediency for political domination and economic exploitation of Korea replaced the value premises underlying an ideal legal system. Arrogance, ruthlessness, execution of the will of the victor, and subjugation of the loser, associated with traditional Japanese martial culture[60] (suicide above surrender) were the foundations of the legal system. Therefore, the prospect of a country-wide nationalist uprising (like the March First Movement of 1919), Japanese sensitivity to world opinion, and the Oriental sense of "face" associated with an inferiority complex toward the Western world were the only limits to the absolute Japanese rule in Korea. Western legal forms and court procedures under Japanese rule were window dressing for the international "face" of Japan. Formal rationality, prominent in Western law, was practically nonexistent.

Under Japanese rule, positive law was composed of three groups of statutory laws: (1) the statutes, orders, and decrees enacted during the last

---

[58] Pak Pyŏng-ho, *Han'guk pŏpchesago, op. cit.* (n. 22), pp. 440–441; *Chosŏn ch'ongdokpu kiguhaesŏl* [On the Organization of the Government of the Governor-General of Korea] (Seoul National University Graduate School of Public Administration, 1960).

[59] There was no institution of judicial review of administrative action. There was no administrative court either. There was only a self-regulatory review institution (*sŏwŏnjedo*) with statutorily limited items of administrative matters within its purview of review.

[60] See Ruth Benedict, *The Chrysanthemum and the Sword*; Maruyama, Masao, *Thought and Behavior in Modern Japanese Politics*, ed. by Ivan Morris (Oxford University Press, expanded edition, 1969), chaps. 1, 2, and 3.

days of the Yi dynasty, which continued in force according to the governor-general's Decree on the Force of Law in Korea of 1910 and the orders and decrees by the Japanese resident-general (1906–1910); (2) the statutes, orders, and decrees of Japan proper which were made applicable to Korea by provisions of the decrees of the governor-general—they did not apply automatically to Korea; and (3) the statutes, orders, and decrees enacted by the governor-general under his authority. The major statutes related to political freedoms that applied to Korea include the Newspaper Law of 1907, the Publication Law of 1909, and the Security Law of 1910. According to these statutes, publication of a newspaper required a publication permit, which depended on the discretion of the government's licensing agency; the decision was not subject to judicial review—there was none. Speech, publishing, newspapers, association, and assembly were subjected to various regulations whenever the broadly worded requirements were met, such as "when public peace and order are disturbed or good morals are harmed" (Publication Law, Arts. 19 and 27; Newspaper Law, Arts. 21 and 26; and Security Law, Art. 4) or "when necessary for the preservation of public peace and order" (Security Law, Art. 1). Any speech or behavior which was "politically disquiet," an equally equivocal requirement, also entailed merciless regulations and punishments (Security Law, Arts. 5, 6, and 7). These regulatory actions were taken entirely at the discretion of policing agencies, likewise without being subject to judicial review. As a matter of legal institutions, therefore, there was no freedom of speech, publication, assembly, and association.

Legislation was made, applied, and executed entirely for administrative requirements and convenience. This point becomes evident in criminal law and procedure. As a law of general application, the Japanese Criminal Law (1907) and Criminal Procedure Law (1890; amended in 1902) also applied to Korea under the authority of the governor-general's Decree on Criminal Matters in Korea of 1912. The Security Law mentioned above, the Law for Punishment of Political Crimes of 1910, the Public Order Maintenance Law of 1925, the Decree on Protective Observation Measures for Thought Criminals of 1936, and the Decree on Preventive Custody Measures for Thought Criminals of 1941, however, prevailed as special laws over the Criminal Law and Criminal Procedures. For that matter alone, therefore, those laws were more important than the Criminal Law and Criminal Procedure Law. Their substantive provisions were defined in broad and vague words, which would endorse their most far-fetched arbitrary interpretation by the police and the prosecutors.[61]

[61] Yi In, a prominent nationalist attorney during the Japanese rule and minister of justice on the establishment of the Korean government, discusses in his memoir various scenes of Japanese administration of justice in Korea. The trial of a case related to a mass popular meeting held in T'ongyŏng (*T'ongyŏng minjungdaehoe sagŏn*) is shown as a mockery of justice. "Naŭi iryŏksŏ" [My Personal History], in *Han'guk Ilbo*, March 16, 1973.

They would hardly pass as laws according to Western notions of justice, such as the rule of law or the doctrine of *nullum crimen, nulla poena, sine lege*. Serious cases were concocted to persecute Korean nationalists.[62]

Job (career) security of judges in Korea was inferior to that of judges in Japan.[63] The judges in Korea did not know judicial review of administrative actions; and they were trained in mechanical, conceptual jurisprudence (or analytic jurisprudence); in their training and outlook they readily accepted administrative actions as legal. Actually, this is part of the civil-law tradition. Almost all judges and public prosecutors in Korea were Japanese.[64] Therefore, judges in Korea readily supported actions taken by the Japanese police and prosecutors against Koreans, especially by arresting Korean nationalists as political criminals.

Statutory provisions and regulations related to Japanese criminal procedure were repugnant to Western notions of justice. No matter how reprehensible was the conduct by the police and the prosecutors in the name of criminal procedure, it was tolerated. There was no requirement to be met before the issuance of a warrant of arrest. A prosecutor was authorized to issue a warrant whenever he deemed it necessary. Under the authority of such a warrant anybody could be placed in custody for an indefinite time. During this time he could lawfully be put to the third degree to get a confession. Under Japanese rule, not only political prisoners but also common criminals were routinely tortured.[65] Thus, an accused was sent to trial half-dead following a long period of investigation under torture conducted by the police, examination by a prosecutor, and another examination by an examining judge before the trial, while in custody in a detention house in extremely poor conditions. It was not unusual that an accused person was maimed or even killed as a result of torture in the process of investigation; death because of torture occurred

[62] As a concocted criminal case, the so-called One Hundred and Five Persons Case of 11 is the most notorious. See Pak Chae-wŏn, "T'anabŭi cheilmak" [The First Scene of Suppression], *Han'guk Hyŏndaesa* [Modern Korean History] (Seoul: Sin'gu munhwasa, 1969), IV, 63–91: *Taehan'guksa* (n. 50), IX, 152–199. See also a levellers case (Hyŏngp'yŏngsa sagŏn—the levellers case—of 1929) as discussed by Yi In in his memoir, "Naŭi iryŏksŏ," in *Han'guk Ilbo*, March 16, 1973.

[63] Pak Pyŏng-ho, *Han'guk pŏpchesago*, pp. 440–441.

[64] See the relevant provisions of the governor-general's Decree on Criminal Matters in Korea and the Japanese Criminal Procedure applied under the authority of the decree. Nam Hŭng-u, "Ilche-ŭi han'guk ch'imryage issŏsŏŭi pŏpkyubŏmgwa kŭ chŏgyonge kwanhanmunje" [Legal Norms and Their Application During the Japanese Aggression of Korea], *Asea Yŏn'gu* [The Journal of Asiatic Studies], 12:1 (1969), 41.

[65] Yi In also gives vivid pictures of brutal torture used to extract confessions during a long imprisonment. Toward the end of the Japanese rule, he himself experienced physical abuses and long imprisonment. See his "Naŭi iryŏksŏ," *Han'guk Ilbo*, March 3, April 4, 6, 7, and 10, 1973.

sometimes even during trial, in prison following trial, or after release from prison.

Under the Japanese criminal system, an innocent person, even a political prisoner having committed no crime beyond being a nationalist, could, curiously enough, be acquitted by the court when his case was found to be concocted by the police. In many cases neither sentence nor acquittal at the trial meant much, especially for political prisoners, because the Japanese goals of intimidating them and Korean society at large were already attained before the trial.[66] The Japanese system of justice was administered with the police at the center.[67] At one time, the Japanese police could lawfully flog Koreans, especially active and potential nationalists, under the authority of the Flogging Decree (1912–1920). The stroke could be weak or strong or lethal.[68] The Flogging Decree was eventually abolished as a "feudal" institution. The Japanese rule of beating, however, was never discarded as a means of torturing and extracting a confession. Under the authority of the mentioned Decree on Protective Observation Measures for Thought Criminals and the Decree on Preventive Custody Measures For Thought Criminals, moreover, blacklisted persons found their freedom of movement curtailed without criminal charge and could be jailed without a trial at the discretion of the police.[69]

Administration of the Western legal system through capitalizing mainly on its criminal law by the police was not simply an exception to the rule even in landlord-tenant and labor disputes.[70] The outstanding trend

[66] Ibid., March 31 and April 10, 1973.

[67] Police power and criminal-law orientation seem best to describe the nature of the legal system under Japanese rule. See also Nam Hŭng-u, *op. cit.* (n. 64), *Asea Yŏn'gu*, XII: (1969), pp. 27–52; Pak Pyŏng-ho, *Han'guk pŏpchesago*, *op. cit.* (n. 22), pp. 433 ff.

[68] Yi Kyu-t'ae shows how the Flogging Decree was implemented. *Kaehwa paekkyŏng* [Hundred Scenes of Modernization] (Seoul: Sint'aeyangsa, 1969), I, 249–251 and 294–301; Pak Pyŏng-ho, *Han'guk pŏpchesago, op. cit.* (n. 22), p. 439.

[69] Kim Tu-hŏn's account of his police imprisonment without trial provides a glimpse of the preventive-custody measures and other Japanese practices with "dangerous" Koreans. Solely because his father was a prominent nationalist leader who had conducted a successful military campaign against Japanese forces in Manchuria, he was taken every three years on an eight-month tour of detention, spending one month in each of the eight police stations of Seoul. He had a total of five such jailhouse tours. *Myŏngin okchunggi* [Prominent Figures' Accounts of Their Jailhouse Experiences] (Seoul: Himangch'ulpansa, 1966), p. 56.

[70] Yi In's experience as an attorney with cases arising from labor and landlord-tenant disputes gives a picture. "Naŭi iryŏksŏ," *Han'guk Ilbo*, March 3 and 14, 1973. See also Kim Yun-hwan, "Hangilŭi p'aŏbilchi: [Diary of Anti-Japanese Strikes], *Han'gukhyŏndaesa*, IV: *Amhŭgŭi sidae* [Dark Period], pp. 424–432; In Chŏng-sik, *Chosŏnŭi t'oji munje* [Land Problems of Korea] (Seoul: Ch'ŏngsusa, 1946), pp. 95–109.

since the cadastration in 1910–1918,[71] which laid the legal foundations of colonial economic exploitation in Korea by introducing modern Roman-law concepts of property rights, was polarization between landlords and sharecroppers, which actually meant polarization between Japanese landlords and Korean sharecroppers. In time, this polarization intensified with the number of independent growers and partly independent, partly sharecropping farmers both decreasing. Among big landlords owning more than 200 *chŏngbo* (500 acres: one *chŏngbo* is 2.45 acres), the number of Japanese landlords increased while that of Korean landlords sharply declined.[72] Besides, Korean landlords were pro-Japanese. Whatever their nationality, landlords were politically and legally protected by the Japanese government in Korea. With harsh rental terms (farmland rent was half the yields in kind or more) and with the Japanese government's measures favorable to landlords, many spontaneous rebellious disputes between sharecroppers and landlords occurred.[73] At the same time, the

[71] As for cadastration, see *Han'gukhak taebaek-kwasajŏn* [Encyclopedia of Korean Studies] (Seoul: Ŭryumunhwasa, 1972), I, 543–545; Yi Sŏn-gŭn, *Taehan'guksa*, IX, pp. 60–103, especially pp. 68 ff.; Kim Yong-sŏp, "Sut'arŭl wihan ch'ŭngnyang-t'ojijosa" [Land Survey for the Purpose of Robbing: The Cadastration], *Han'gukhyŏndaesa*, IV, 96–130.

[72] *Han'gukhak taebaek-kwasajŏn, op. cit.* (n. 71), I, 544; Chŏn Sŏk-tam, Yi Ki-su, and Kim Han-ju, Ilchehaŭi chosŏnsahoegyŏngjesa [Social and Economic History of Korea under the Japanese Rule] (Seoul: Chogŭmnyŏn, 1947), p. 30, Chu Chong-hang, "Ssari ŏmnŭn chŭngsan" [Rice Production Growth Without Rice], *Han'gukhyŏndaesa*, IV, 140; In Chŏng-sik, *Chosŏnŭi t'oji munje, op. cit.* (n. 70), pp. 91–96; In Chŏng-sik, *Chosŏn nongŏp kyŏngjeron* [On Korean Agricultural Economy] (Seoul: Pangmunch'ulp'ansa, 1949), p. 54; Yi Ki-baek, Kuksasillon [A New Korean History] (Seoul: Cheil ch'ulp'ansa, 1963), pp. 347–348; Yi Hong-jik et al., *Kuksa sin'gang* [A New Korean History] (Seoul: Ilchogak, 1958), pp. 419–421; Boku Bunse, Noson shakai bunka no kuten to shite no tochi chosa jigyo ni tsuite" [Land Survey as the Turning Point of Village Social Structure], *Chosen shakaikeizaishi kenkyu* [Studies on Korean Social and Economic History] (Seoul: Keijo Imperial University Law Association, 1933), pp. 521–567; Pak Mun-gyu, *Chosŏn t'oji munje non'go* [On Land Problems in Korea] (Seoul: Chosŏninminbosa, 1946), p. 54; Yi Yŏng-hyŏp, *Han'guk kŭndae t'oji chedosa yŏn'gu* [A Study of the History of Korean Land Tenure System] (Seoul: Pomungak, 1968), pp. 146–147; Pak Pyŏng-hong, *Han'guk nongŏp saengsallon* [On Korean Agricultural Production] (Seoul: Indaesa, 1974), p. 86; Kim Mun-sik et al, *Ilcheŭi kyŏngje ch'imt'alsa* [History of Japanese Economic Exploitation] (Seoul: Minjungsŏgwan, 1971), pp. 1–109, especially pp. 34–35.

[73] In 1922, there were 24 recorded cases of landlord-tenant disputes in which 2,539 persons participated; in 1925, 204 cases with 4,002 participants; and in 1930, 726 cases with 13,012 participants. See Yi Ki-baek, *op. cit.* (n. 72), p. 358; Yi Yŏng-hyŏp, *op. cit.* (n. 72), p. 186–190; Yi Hun-gu, *Chosŏn nongŏmnon* [On Korean Agriculture] (Seoul: Hansŏng tosŏ chusikhoesa, 1935); Pak Pyŏng-hong, *op. cit.* (n. 72), pp. 89–92; Tsumagari Kuranjo, "Chosen ni okeru kosaku mondai no hatten katei" [Development of Tenant Problems in Korea], *Chosen keizai no*

spread of socialist ideas and nationalist ideologies among peasants also contributed to landlord-tenant disputes. Those disputes were a form of socialist and nationalist sentiment, albeit subdued, and the problems which caused them could not be solved as long as the Japanese dominated Korea. Similar circumstances caused labor disputes. In the 1920s and 1930s, Japanese capitalists began to build military industries in Korea where labor and raw materials were cheap. The number of industrial workers increased. Labor disputes arose, caused by demands for wage increases and abolition of ethnic discrimination.[74] The Japanese paid low wages, demanded long working hours, and introduced harsh labor terms. They also discriminated against Korean workers, paying them half of what they paid Japanese workers for the same work. Socialist and nationalist stirrings contributed to the labor disputes as they did to landlord-tenant disputes.

Those disputes were subdued by the police who arrested the leaders, then released some of them with warnings or torturing them in the investigation. The rest had to stand criminal trial. The disputes were not judicially resolved as civil matters, not even in the interest of landlords and employers and against tenants and workers. There were no labor laws, nor laws advancing the rights of tenants. Only those aspects of the disputes that affected peace and order were acknowledged by the Japanese rulers.

The laws under Japanese rule were enacted according to the requirements of the colonial rulers. The laws embodied neither principles and rules of Western public law nor a system of moral norms to restrain the rulers. An example of how these laws were applied in civil-law matters is the Rules for Execution of Mortgages on House and Lands, enacted in 1906 specifically to protect Japanese loan sharks.[75] The rules provided for

---

kenkyu [Studies of Korean Economy] (Seoul: Keijo Imperial University Law Association, 1929), II, 289–428, especially 397 ff.

[74] There were only 10,000 factory and mine workers in 1912, but the number reached 140,000 in 1931, 270,000 in 1937, and 730,000 in 1943. The number of labor disputes also increased annually. There were 6 recorded cases in which 1,573 persons participated in 1912, 36 cases with 3,403 participants in 1921, 180 participants in 1931. Demands for wage increases and improvement of labor conditions were the major issues of those disputes. Labor conditions were extremely poor. About 47 percent of the factory workers and 34 percent of the mine workers worked more than twelve hours a day. The average wage of Korean workers was less than half of that of Japanese workers. See Yamada Fumio, "Chosenjin rōdōsha mondai" [Labor Problems of Korean Workers], *Chosen keizaino kenkyu* [Study of Korean Economy], pp. 429–542, especially pp. 434 ff.; Yi ki-baek, *op. cit.* (n. 72), pp. 364–365; Kim Yun-hwan, "Hangilŭi p'aŏbilchi," *op. cit.* (n. 70), IV, 402–448.

[75] *Han'gukhak taebaek-kwasajŏn, op. cit.* (n. 71), p. 542.

the right of the mortgagee to take as forfeit without further procedure mortgaged properties upon the default of the mortgagor when the right was reserved in the contract. This rule was contrary to the provisions of the Japanese Civil Code, which specifically prohibited such a forfeiture. Again, according to these rules, a creditor (mortgagee) was entitled to sell mortgaged properties by bidding in the presence of the village head, chief of a subdistrict (*myŏn*), or two male adults as witnesses, upon the default of a debtor (mortgagor), without going through the otherwise required procedure of judicial sale as provided by the Japanese Civil Code.

The cadastration conducted under the authority of the Cadastration Decree (1921) stands as a turning point in the introduction of modern (Roman) concepts of property rights to Korean society. As the results of cadastration, the Koreans woke up one morning to find that the government of the governor-general had come to own legally 44 percent of the entire area of Korea. The Western sense of justice requires that vested rights be legally protected and that procedural requirements, including the right to be heard in a court of law, be met to determine legal relationship between parties. The cadastration was done in disregard of such basic Western notions. Property rights in the cadastration work were determined on the basis of reports filed by the individual owners, many of whom were illiterate and unfamiliar with a modern report system. Partly out of ignorance, partly because of a rumor that high taxes would follow the report, and partly from a nationalist attitude of noncooperation, many lands went unreported; these were seized by the governor-general as unclaimed. Moreover, the traditional concepts of property relations did not neatly fit into the modern (Roman) concepts of property rights. It was quite possible that a number of persons owned the same piece of land, not as co-owners but in a different order; for example, one with the right to collect rents and another with the right to cultivate. Yet what they both owned was inherited generation after generation. Therefore, it was not easy to determine who owned what according to modern concepts. Nevertheless, the cadastration work was implemented in disregard of the niceties of the traditional ownership concepts while the rights to collect rent alone were recognized. As a result, the upper classes were generally favored among Koreans. And those lands from which government offices were entitled to collect rent were turned over to government ownership. (In old Korea, government agencies drew their revenue also from rents collected from farmers who currently *owned* the lands from which they held the right to collect rent.) Consequently, the farming masses were deprived of the lands they had cultivated as their own lands for generations. They were now reduced to rent-paying sharecroppers on the lands of their ancestors. Furthermore, the determination of owners and other related actions, including surveying and title-recording, were made entirely by administrative action of which there was no judicial review. Large portions of the lands thus determined to be government-owned were sold for nominal fees to such big land-owning Japanese corporations as *Tōyō Takushoku Kaisha* (a Japanese version of the British East India Company) and to individual Japanese colonists. Those landowning corporations and individual colonists became the rent-collecting landlords over the Korean sharecropper masses. By cadastration the Japanese systematically reorganized Korea's society into a society composed of two classes, landlords and sharecroppers.

With this picture of criminal law and police-power-oriented Western law and Korean society under Japanese rule, it is not difficult to imagine that a legal profession, composed of mostly Japanese judges and prosecutors, and of Korean and Japanese practicing lawyers, had little say in terms of their role conducive to the growth of a middle class or to the autonomy of law. The judge dominated the court proceedings because its procedure was inquisitorial. A humanitarian lawyer at best could raise only extenuating circumstances as a defense or simply appeal to the judge's compassion on behalf of a Korean criminal defendant. Many Japanese and Korean lawyers were reluctant to defend Korean political criminals or did a perfunctory job when they accepted the appointment. Consequently, a few Korean nationalist lawyers easily stood out among others by bravely accepting an unpopular appointment and vigorously defending.

Because of the presence of the few Korean nationalist lawyers, the legal profession was instrumental in transmitting the image of the traditional magistrate as just and as a rectifier of wrongs to the modern legal profession, and in transmitting the universal values associated with the royal examination to the modern bar examination. As with the latter factor, legal and medical professions were the only professions which able Koreans could aspire to with a fair chance.[76] Once becoming a lawyer, one could fight for a Korean cause against the Japanese rule with relative impunity among other professions. In any case, the legal profession also left an image of its role subservient to the power.

Remnants of Japanese imperialist colonial rule still persist in some areas of government organizations today. Under Japanese rule, the positions that were allowed to be held by Koreans in the government and government-related public and private organizations were at best those of medium managerial level.[77] As a result of the systematic implementation

[76] See note 77.

[77] Koreans were systematically barred from becoming trained administrators,

of Japanese policies on illiteracy that foreclosed to Koreans opportunities to have a higher education and advanced training, those Koreans who manned the lowest strata of the Japanese colonial government organization were the only trained and experienced persons able to run modern administrative offices, the police, the army, the courts, and even the prisons, when the Japanese left Korea after Korean liberation at the end of the Second World War. They were now appointed to high positions in the hierarchies of the newly formed government. They formed the core elements of various branches of government, and their influence was decisive in the formation of governmental organizations and in the recruitment and training of new generations of officers and personnel. A number of pro-Japanese Koreans and even those who were members of the notorious political sections of the Japanese police (whose main function was to detect Korean nationalists) found their way into high posts of practically every field of public activities—legislation, administration, judiciary, police, army, and education. Following the establishment of a new government, the Special Examination Committee of Anti-National Acts (1948) was formed under strong popular pressure to prosecute those pro-Japanese Koreans who had committed "malicious anti-national acts" under Japanese rule. From the beginning, however, the committee encountered governmental opposition ranging from noncooperation to obstruction, so that its goals had to be largely abandoned; only a few offenders were punished. Generous treatment of most pro-Japanese Koreans was dictated by the circumstances. The police and the military which were necessary to maintain public order against rampaging Communist subversives would have been critically demoralized if a large

---

managers, engineers, scientists, and social scientists. Only 20 percent of the Korean population had a formal education under the Japanese when Korea was liberated (Gregory Henderson, *Korea: The Politics of the Vortex* [Cambridge: Harvard University Press, 1968], p. 89). Yu Chin-o, who studied Western science of law at the Keijo Imperial University (the only university founded by the Japanese in Korea) was the top student of his class for four years, but was denied professorship only because he was a Korean. Upon liberation, he greatly contributed to the constitutional framework of Korea. He was a long-time president of Korea University and once became the leader of the opposition party. See his memoir "P'yŏnp'yŏn yahwa" (Night-time Stories), *Dong-a Ilbo*, March 29 and 30, 1974.

The only professions accessible to Koreans under Japanese rule were lawyers and medical doctors. Only about a fifth of the judges, a tenth of the prosecutors, half of the clerks, and none of the bailiffs were Koreans. Only in private practice did the number of Koreans generally match that of the Japanese. See the following table:

Year	Judges		Prosecutors		Apprentice Judges or Prosecutors		Practicing Lawyers		Bailiffs		Clerks and Interpreters	
	Japanese	Korean	Japanese	Korean	Japanese	Korean	Japanese	Korean	Japanese	Korean	Japanese	Korean
1909	218	111	78	7	0	...	...	...	...	...	298	257
1910	183	71	54	6	...	...	30	51	1	0	...	...
1917	160	37	54	10	...	...	74	94	23	2	377	197
1925	150	33	66	9	4	1	143	166	65	0	467	209
1931	165	33	78	9	...	...	156	210	84	0	501	209
1934	152	41	79	7	20	5	169	209	88	0	497*	217*
1935	146	38	74	7	14	4	172	217	88	0	491*	222*

SOURCE: *Chosen Nenkan*, 1934, 1937, and 1938 editions.
... indicates that figures are not available.
* shows only the number of clerks and does not include interpreters.

number of former Japanese collaborators had been expelled.[78] Some Japanese remnants remain in the police to this day. Japanese attitudes of varying degrees can be still spotted in many fields of law making, implementing and applying.[79]

THE PRESENT LEGAL SYSTEM OF KOREA

Korea owes its liberation from Japanese rule to the victory of the Allied Forces over Japan in the Second World War. Korea, a culturally homogenous and politically unified entity for many centuries, came to be divided, however, into two parts along the 38th parallel and placed under the military authorities of the two world powers, the U.S. and the U.S.S.R. One consequence was that two distinctive forms of government reflecting those of the occupying powers were set up, a democratic government in the South and a Communist system in the North. Thereafter, two different models of social transformation were pursued under the two systems, a Western model of society in the South and a Stalinist Soviet model in the North. Two different legal systems emerged, drastically departing from their common past. A discussion of the North Korean legal system is beyond the scope of this discussion. The legal system of South Korea alone will be considered.

It was only in South Korea that Koreans were allowed to determine their own fate. After a brief period of joy after the liberation, Korea's society lapsed into political chaos. All colors of the political spectrum from the far right to the far left competed for political dominance. The world powers proposed a United Nations trusteeship for all of Korea, but the proposal was met by vehement Korean opposition as humiliation. Meanwhile, Communists in the North supported subversive activities in the South. Many Korean political leaders desired the immediate establishment of a government in the South, while others wanted national unification first. Finally, a Western democratic form of government emerged in the South following a general election under United Nations auspices. But major problems and tasks remained. The Korean War followed (1950–1953) and its aftermath, including reconstruction from wartime destruction, democratic experiments (1960),[80] a military *coup*

[78] *Han'guksa taegye* [Outline of the History of Korea], IX (1973), 65–66; *Han'gukhak taepaek-kwasajŏn, op. cit.* (N. 71), I, 245; Yi In, "Naŭi iryŏksŏ," *Han'guk Ilbo*, May 5, 1973.

[79] The remarks of Sŏ Min-ho, one of the political opposition leaders, about his prison experiences under Japanese rule and under the Rhee regime are interesting. See *Myŏngin okchunggi, op. cit.* (n. 69), chapter on Sŏ Min-ho, especially pp. 112 and 117 ff.

[80] See Han Sung-joo, *The Failure of Democracy in South Korea* (Berkeley: University of California Press, 1974).

d'état (1961), and rapid industrialization with its related political, social, and economic problems in the late 1960s and 1970s. The North Korean regime under Kim Il-sŏng's one-man dictatorship along with its avowed policy of a South Korean takeover posed itself as a continuous threat to the survival of the South as a democratic entity and a cause for economic and human suffering in terms of military preparations in the South and North; national unification has been the dominating national goal in Korean consciousness.

It seems again important to discuss the legal system in historical continuity. The present system is best seen as an expression of the Korean reaction to Japanese rule. As we have seen, the basis of the Western formal legal structure was laid down by the Japanese. The present system constitutes a drastic departure from the Japanese model. The departure was intentional on the part of the Korean elite, mainly the legal profession, legal scholars, and political leaders. Any institution or practice reminiscent of the Japanese was rejected. Thus, the deliberate departure from the Japanese past resulted in a move from one end of the spectrum of Western law to the other–from the law as a means of repression and subjugation, guided neither by a moral system nor by public law, to the law that incorporates the romanticized Western ideal of liberal and social democratic norms.

Korea's political determination for her future including her departure from the Japanese past to reach the goal of a Western democratic society is expressed in the constitution of 1948 (and thereafter). From the preamble and the provisions of this constitution, we deduce three themes: (1) a nationalist vision of independence and self-determination; (2) a Western liberal democracy; and (3) a social-democratic ideal. These three themes are reflected in the three words of the constitution's preamble, *independence, liberty*, and *social justice*. Independence and freedom were the ideological themes that Koreans had cherished throughout Japanese rule, as shown in the Declaration of Independence of the March 1st Movement (1919) and the constitution of the Korean government in exile in China (1919). The Western world's trend toward socialism (or the welfare state) within a democratic institutional framework also left its mark on the Korean political system.

A new generation of legal scholars and lawyers who do not understand Japanese has been growing up. Many of these men were trained in Western countries. Their comparative studies yielded scholarly inspiration and practical guidance. American influence and postwar experiences in the civil-law countries found their expression in legislative and scholarly works. As Korea is industrializing, it is faced with such problems as pollution, communications, transportation, urban planning, redevelopment of slum areas, sanitation, and public health. But comparative studies in the Western countries have resulted in copying with little adaptation Western ways for quick solutions of the problems. Only recently have Koreans begun to become aware that copying alone does not give satisfactory solutions. Societies have many features in common and differ in other features. What is Korea's national identity and what is its legal expression?

Korea's constitution, first adopted in 1948, was amended several times (in 1952, 1954, 1960, 1962, 1969, and 1972). A number of important constitutional experiments were accordingly conducted in the meantime. Even when practically a new constitution was adopted in 1962, and again in 1972, however, the adoption consciously took the form of amendments. Thus, basic major continuities prevail. There is continuity in the three ideological themes. Many provisions remain essentially as they were initially worded in the constitution of 1948. Changes are relatively minor ones, adopted to accommodate the changing political groups. The amendments are largely related to particular forms of government within the broad framework of liberal democratic political institutions.

(1) As a nationalist expression, the constitution, which explicitly prohibited enactment of *ex post facto* penal statutes and contained many other liberal democratic features, made an exception authorizing the enactment of a special law providing for the punishment of "malicious anti-national acts" committed before August 15, 1945 (Art. 101). We have seen, however (p. 85), that the goal of the special Law for the Punishment of Anti-National Acts (1948) could not be fully attained. Another expression of nationalism is the codification[81] designed to replace by Korean codes all Japanese laws, decrees, orders, and regulations (and the American military decrees proclaimed during the U.S. military administration after the Japanese defeat), which remained temporarily in force under the constitution. The codification work took ten years. Thus, the Criminal Code (1953), the Criminal Procedure Law (1954), the Civil Code (1958), the Civil Procedure Law (1960), and the Commercial Code (1962), and others were adopted; they contained special features designed to express their separateness from the previous Japanese codes.

The nationalist measures eliminating Japanese and restoring Korean elements also included a wide range of other matters, such as names of persons, streets, and towns (Japanese-style names had been imposed during Japanese rule), use of Korean as the official language, prohibition of the use of the Japanese language, bans on Japanese songs and books, adoption of a different calendar, and a different local standard time. The constitutional principle of popular sovereignty (Art. 2; presently Art. 1,

[81] See Yi In, "Naŭi iryŏksŏ," *Han'guk Ilbo*, March 3, 1973; Special Law for the Replacement of Old Statutes and Orders of July 15, 1961.

Sec. 2) is not merely a protest against sovereign power held by the monarch as in the West but also a nationalist expression of self-determination against foreign rule.

National unification looms as the principal goal, although the chance of realization is slim in the near future. National unification was not mentioned in the previous constitutions—the goal appeared too obvious to Koreans to be written into the constitution. The goal finally finds its most pronounced expression in the provisions of the present constitution, adopted in December, 1972 (Preamble, Arts. 35, 37 Sec. 1, 38, and 43 Sec. 3), following the South-North dialogues of early 1972. In the South, the Korean War, the confrontation and tension between South and North, and threats from the North are perceived in fratricidal terms whereas in the North they are defined in terms of Communist "liberation of the South." The threats from the North and the tensions between the two Koreas exact a heavy toll in human and economic costs and also in terms of constitutional and legal measures necessary for the survival of South Korea as a democracy. The measures for the system's survival include emergency power of the executive, martial law, and other restrictions placed on the exercise of individual freedoms and rights. Incidentally, the constitution is visualized as being valid throughout all Korea. Constitutionally, the South Korean government has been the only legitimate government with an endorsement by the United Nations in the form of recognition by the General Assembly. Under the constitution, the North Korean regime is at best a belligerent group in conventional international-law terms.

(2) In 1948, as the result of liberal democratic determination, a liberal democratic constitution which had the features of Western liberal democracies was adopted in Korea. In view of the long-cherished Korean aspiration for freedom from Japanese rule, victory of democracy, and the presence of the American military administration, the constitution could not be otherwise than liberal and democratic. Western liberal democracy finds its legal expression, apart from the constitution of 1948 (and subsequently adopted constitutions), in the statutory codes enacted under its authority, including particularly the Criminal Procedure Law. The present Korean legal system is characterized by its public-law elements, just as the legal system under Japanese rule was characterized by its lack of public law. The present legal system is composed of both public law and *imperium* elements. As in the West, the Korean legal system is a formal rational system.

A comment on the democratic characteristics of the constitution may be in order. As written, the Korean constitution is one of the liberal democratic constitutional documents in the world, both too Western and too liberal to be realistic under prevailing political, social, and economic conditions. The most liberal constitutional documents, the American,

German (both Weimar and present West German), English, and French constitutions, especially the first two, decisively influenced the Korean constitution. Following the April Student Uprising in 1960, for instance, a Korean experiment with parliamentary liberal democracy was undertaken with the constitution adopted in that year, which provided for a full-fledged parliamentary form of government together with a constitutional court of the German type as an institution of judicial review of legislation. The democratic experience ended as a fiasco, however, with a military *coup d'état* in 1961, which followed the power vacuum after the fall of the Syngman Rhee regime. For another example, the Korean constitution provided for the citizen's constitutional right of tort liability of the government, allowing no sovereign immunity or exception—a tort rule which even American law has not fully incorporated. The North Korean military challenge necessitated South Korean defensive military preparations. With 600,000 men in the armed forces and general compulsory military duty, the number of military personnel killed or injured negligently by fellow soldiers in an army compound or a maneuver is large. Since a negligent act on the part of a soldier legally constituted a tort of the government, the injured or their family could claim damages from the government, which became a huge drain on the governmental budget already strained by other commitments. The professional interests of practicing lawyers were also partly responsible for an upsurge of tort claims against the government in the 1960s. Consequently, the government introduced a statutory measure that exempted military personnel from government tort liability. A significant number of lower-court decisions, however, declared the statutory provision unconstitutional in the 1960s. Finally, the Supreme Court declared the statutory provision unconstitutional as repugnant to the equal-protection-of-law clause.[82] The

[82] Supreme Court Judgment 22.6.1971 (70 Ta 1010). This judgment actually includes two Supreme Court rulings: The first, that the exception to the rule of government tort liability against military personnel was unconstitutional, in violation of the equal-protection clause. (It was a 9 to 7 decision; the Supreme Court of Korea is composed of 16 Justices.) This ruling would not have been possible without the second ruling that accompanied the first in that same judgment. As a means of discouraging judicial review, a statutory measure was introduced in 1970 to make it necessary to have an affirmative vote of two-thirds of the Justices for the Supreme Court to declare a statute unconstitutional instead of a simple majority. The second ruling struck the statutory two-thirds requirement as an unconstitutional restraint of the power of the Supreme Court by an 11 to 5 vote. Without this second ruling, the first ruling was short two votes. Both rulings, however, were reversed by the constitutional amendments in 1972. The military exception to the rule of governmental tort liability and the two-thirds vote requirement in constitutional ruling are now parts of the provisions of the Constitution of 1972. In the same reverse trend, the first ruling was specifically overruled by the Supreme Court in 1977. And yet the institution of judicial review remains a part of the constitution today. See Dai-Kwon Choi, *Law and Social Change: The Korean*

constitutional rulings and the subsequent "judicial crisis"[83] were partly responsible for the introduction of the constitutional order of 1972. Under this constitution, governmental powers are strengthened by several crisis government provisions whereas the bills of human civil rights retreated to some extent. For instance, the provisions of *habeas corpus* were phased out under the present constitution of 1972.

Korea's constitutional history is a history of constitutional amendments. By way of these amendments, experiments have been made with both classic parliamentary and presidential forms of government (1960–1961) and with two derivative forms of the presidential system, one close to the Weimar system (1948–1960) and the other close to the French Fifth Republic's system (since 1972). Experiments have also been made with different forms of judicial review of legislation, an American form of judicial review (1962–1972), a constitutional court on the German model, and two Korean-created institutions of judicial review, the Constitutional Committee, a hybrid of the French Constitutional Council, the German Constitutional Court, and American judicial review but rather close to the second (1948–1960 and 1972). Under the institution of 1948–1960, two rulings by the Constitutional Committee that declared a statutory provision[84] unconstitutional and another ruling by the same Committee

---

Experience (doctoral dissertation, University of California, Berkeley, 1976), pp. 221–227 and 247–249.

[83] Kim Ch'ŏl-su, *Hŏnbŏphak* [Science of Constitutional Law] (Seoul: Chihaksa, 1972), pp. 940–1053; Dai-Kwon Choi, *Law and Social Change* (n. 82), pp. 227–240.

[84] Constitutional Committee (which had the power of judicial review of legislation, 1948–1960) Decision 8.10.1952 (1952 Hŏnsim 1) and Constitutional Committee Decision 9.9.1952 (1952 Hŏnsim 2). *Chusŏk han'guk p'anllyejip* [Annotated Case Reports of Korea], published by the Korea Law Research Institute, Seoul National University, Public Law, Part 1, pp. 16–19. The two cases in which a statute was declared unconstitutional were grounded on the constitutional "right to have a trial conducted in conformity with the law by judges qualified under the Constitution and law" (Art. 22). The Committee ruled that the right included a right to appeal to the Supreme Court as the court of last resort. But the Land Reform Law of 1949 (Art. 18, Sec. 1, 2nd paragraph and Art. 24, Sec. 1, 2nd paragraph) made the court of second instance the final court for a dispute arising from land reform. And Article 9 of the Extraordinary Measure Ordinance in Emergency (having the force of a statute as a wartime emergency measure to fight crimes following the outbreak of the Korean War in 1950), provided for a trial conducted by a single-judge court of a district court without appeal for the crimes defined by the Ordinance and allowed a retrial conducted by a three-judge panel of a district court only to those who were sentenced to death or life imprisonment. The Land Reform Law and the Extraordinary Measure Ordinance were declared in violation of the constitutional provision for the right to trial. Both rulings were handed down when civil rights were under a severe strain in a most hostile environment immediately following the Korean War.

were constitutionally significant.[85] Under the American institution of 1962–1972 the Supreme Court declared the statutory exemption of military personnel from the application of the constitutional rule of the government's tort liability unconstitutional. These performances are outstanding for the thirty-year history of Korea's constitution under unfavorable political, social, and economic conditions as compared with, say, the performance of Japanese judicial review.[86] It is difficult to say,

[85] Constitutional Committee Decision 8.10.1953 (1953 Hŏnsim 2), *Chusŏk han'guk p'anllyejip*, pp. 8–11. In the decision, the Constitutional Committee took a self-restraining position that it cannot impute to the government any intention of violating a constitutional provision unless it is clearly spelled out. Although it did not declare a statutory provision unconstitutional, however, the committee by this ruling frustrated the government's real intention. The government arrested a person with an arrest warrant issued by a public prosecutor, not by a judge, on the basis of the Martial Law Act Article 13, because its issuance was initially refused by a district court judge. The validity of the arrest was challenged by the defendant on the ground that the Martial Law Act Article 13 violated Article 9 of the constitution which provided for a warrant. The committee's ruling was that the "special measure" of the Martial Law Act Article 13 could not be interpreted to include arrest without a warrant issued by a judge, and therefore, the Martial Law Act Article 13 was constitutional. CC. Decision 29.3.1952 (1951 Hŏnsim 1, 2) and CC Decision 26.3.1954 (1954 Hŏnsim 1) may be cited as other examples. Chusŏk han'guk p'anllye, Public Law Part, pp. 3–6 and pp. 20–21. This pattern of judicial self-restraint–in which a ruling declaring a statute in issue unconstitutional is avoided and yet the government's unconstitutional legislative intention is thwarted by way of resorting to a strict statutory interpretation–was followed during the 1962–1972 period by the Supreme Court in a number of cases where the state interests collided with the constitutionally protected individual rights (interests). During the period, the Supreme Court was the court of last resort that had the power of judicial review of legislation under an American style judicial review system. See SC Judgment 18.7.1967 (65 Nu 172); SC Judgment 18.2.1969 (68 To 1846); SC Judgment 23.12.1969 (68 To 1831); SC Judgment 29.1.1970 (69 Ta 1203), Pŏmnyul sinmun (Law Weekly: Feb. 9, 1970), and *Taebŏbwŏn p'an'gyŏlchip* (Supreme Court Law Reports: CivR 18.1.47–51); SC Judgment 10.2.1970 (19 Ta 1729), and *Taebŏbwŏn p'an'gyŏlchip* (CivR 18.1.76–78); SC Judgment 24.2.1970 (69 Ta 1069), *Taebŏbwŏn p'an'gyŏlchip* (CivR 18.1.116–117).

[86] In the thirty years of Japanese constitutional history since the end of the Second World War, there is only one constitutional ruling in which a statutory provision was declared by the Supreme Court. The ruling, handed down by the Supreme Court in 1973, was on the validity of the Criminal Code Article 200 prescribing punishment mandatorily heavier for patricide (capital or life imprisonment) than for ordinary murder (capital, life imprisonment, and more than three years of imprisonment). See Supreme Court Judgment 4.4.1973: S. Ct. Crim. Reports Vol. 27, No. 3, p. 265. In Japan, as in Korea, where Confucian tradition is still strong, patricide has been regarded as one of the most heinous crimes entailing heaviest punishment. Thus, the wisdom and the constitutional validity of Article 200 has been subjected to serious doubt only in recent years. Its val-

however, whether the present retreat from liberalism is a digression from the road to liberalism or a maximum which presently Korean society could realistically achieve under its various countervailing historical, political, social, and economic conditions. At least partly responsible for the retreat are the threats from North Korea, the fear of American military withdrawal, the leadership of the government in industrialization and the solution of political and socioeconomic problems, and the stability needed for concerted efforts.

The emerging sign of constitutionalism is to a great extent associated with a growing legal profession. The size of the legal profession has grown considerably following the end of the Second World War, although the percentage of lawyers in the population lags far behind that of other countries, especially that of England and the United States.[87] The presence of a legal profession is undoubtedly conducive to the growth of autonomy of law and of constitutionalism. Besides, Korea's economic growth provided a favorable environment to constitutionalism. Economic resources

---

idity was previously confirmed in 1950 by the Supreme Court's constitutional ruling (Supreme Court Judgment 11.10.1950: S. Ct. Crim. Reports Vol. 4, No. 10, p. 2037). The 1973 constitutional ruling was hailed as a relief to the concern that the Japanese institution of judicial review was defunct. It was hailed as the first one in which the Supreme Court asserted its power to judicially review legislation rather than one in which a tradition-bound criminal provision was struck down as violating the equal-protection-of-law clause. But the case was unusual; a daughter expecting to marry killed her incestuous father after he repeatedly beat her and obstructed her marriage. The unusually strong moral implications of the case made the irrationality in the provision particularly glaring. It is difficult to tell whether the outrageous nature of the case or the constitutional validity of the provision charged as violating the equal-protection -of-law clause contributed to the constitutional ruling. The Japanese institution of judicial review follows the American model. Unlike West Germany's Constitutional Court, the Supreme Court of the United States is empowered to make a constitutional ruling only in the process of performing its adjudicatory function in a particular case or controversy, and any statement made by the Supreme Court on issues not raised in the case or controversy is an *obiter dictum.* A majority of eight Justices thought that the great disparity in punishment between patricide and an ordinary murder was too much, whereas six Justices regarded the distinction in punishment between patricide and ordinary murder as being of a constitutionally irrational nature. The decision was fourteen to one. See Hirano Ryuichi, "Sonzoku satsujin iken hanketsu ni tsuite" [Concerning the Constitutional Ruling on Patricide], *Horitsu jiho*, 45:5 (April, 1973), 55–57; *Kempō hanrei hyakusen* [One Hundred Constitutional Cases] 3rd edition, *Bessatu* [special issue of] *Juristo*, No. 44 (June, 1974), pp. 22–23, with comment by Kojima Kazushi.

[87] For a brief comparative statistical picture of lawyers in major countries, see Marc Galanter, "Introduction: The Study of the Indian Legal Profession," *Law and Society Review*, 3:2 (1969), 204–205; Ch'oe Kwang-yul, "Pyŏnhosasilt'ae-e Kwanhan T'onggye punsŏk" (A Statistical Analysis of Practicing Lawyers), *Pyŏnhosa* (Practicing Lawyers), 9 (1978), 92.

tend to make people more likely to resort to legal means to protect their political and social as well as economic interests. Further, a growing economy produces a greater need for legal services. The rapidly grown volume of Korea's international trade which occasioned a special need for legal experts in international transactions is an example in point. Also pertinent is liberal education in Korea, which has been a vehicle to instill liberal values since 1945.

(3) The Constitution of 1948 initially envisioned a socialist or mixed economic and social order guided by the goal of "social justice," which would be attained by "fulfilling the basic requirements of all citizens" and by "development of a balanced national economy." An individual's economic freedom was to be "guaranteed within these limits." For the envisioned economic and social order, the Weimar Constitution was the model. The protection of property rights was explicitly spelled out in the constitution, and payment of "just compensation in accordance with the provisions of law" was constitutionally made necessary in case of eminent domain. The emphasis was, however, on the institutional nature of the private-property system. Far from being an absolute right, private property became a right whose "contents and restrictions shall be defined by law"; private property was further viewed as carrying inherent restrictions placed on it to conform to "the welfare of the public."

Accordingly, the constitution of 1948 provided for distribution of farmlands to the tillers (Art. 86), but the property rights to the farmlands acquired under the authority of the Land Reform Law of 1948 are such that farmer-owners cannot lease their farmlands or let others cultivate them; moreover, a farming household cannot hold more than 3 *chŏngbo* (7.35 acres) of farmlands. Farmer-owners can sell farmlands thus acquired but only upon sanction of the local authority (even after payment of compensation owed to the government at the time of their acquisition). Farmlands thus acquired can be inherited. The constitution of 1948 provided, furthermore, "mines and other important underground resources, marine resources, water power and all other economically available natural powers shall be owned by the state" (Art. 84), and "important transportation, communication, banking, insurance, electricity, water utility, water service, gas and other enterprises of public utility shall be run by the state or the public" (Art. 87). These provisions complemented a list of "social rights" as indispensable ingredients of the fundamental human rights in the constitution of 1948. They included provisions for equal opportunities of education, compulsory elementary education (Art. 16), the right and duty to work (Art. 17, Sec. 1), the standards of labor conditions (Art. 17, Sec. 2), special protection for working women and children (Art. 17, Sec. 3), freedoms of association, collective bargaining and collective action of laborers (Art. 18, Sec. 1), workers' right to share in the profits of profit-earning private enterprises (Art. 18, Sec. 2), governmental protection for the aged, sick, and others (Art. 19), a marriage institution based on sexual equality, and the governmental protection accorded to the purity of marriage and the health of the family (Art. 20).

The socialist or mixed economic and social order envisioned in the constitution is also a natural Korean reaction to their grim experiences under Japanese rule. The first task undertaken by the newly established Korean government was the land reform. Lands owned by absentee landlords and by the former landlords were distributed to tillers, and the landlords as a dominating socioeconomic class disappeared from the Korean social scene. To some extent this social order was caused by the trend toward socialism in the Western world following the two world wars, and by the presence of the Communist world in general and the North Korean Communists in particular. As for Korea, which did not have a sizable industrial base, the constitutionally envisioned economic and social order was more than revisionary of capitalism; it was a blueprint for the construction of a future socioeconomic order in Korea.

As in many countries of the Third World, industrialization has been one of the most pressing national goals. Between the two models of economic development available today, the historical domestic and international conditions left no choice but to take the model of market economy, with the Soviet model ruled out. It did not take long for the Korean elite to realize that the economic and social order envisioned by the constitution of 1948 was too much tilted toward socialism or statism requiring great involvement of the state while leaving little room for individual initiative. They worried that this social order might hinder economic growth by scaring off prospective private investment. Thus, in 1954 and 1962 constitutional amendments were adopted to move further toward a free market economy. Since 1962 the leading principle for economic and social order has become that of "respect for freedom and creative ideas of the individual in economic affairs" (Constitution of 1962, Art. 111 Sec. 1; Constitution of 1972, Art. 116, Sec. 2). The provision of the constitution of 1948, Article 85, was accordingly deleted from the constitution of 1954, and the constitution of 1948, Article 87, was replaced in 1954 by the provision that "private enterprises shall not be transferred to the state or to public ownership, except in cases specifically designated by law to meet the urgent necessities of national defense or national life, nor shall their management or operation be controlled by the state or by any juridical person organized by public law" (Constitution of 1954, Art. 88.) The right of workers to share in the profits of private enterprises was also deleted from the constitution in 1962 and thereafter.

The thus formulated economic and social order, based on the free market model, has been the framework of economic activities in which the industrialization of Korea has evolved. In less than two decades starting from the middle of the 1960s, the Korean gross national product has grown more than ten times, and the industrial base has enormously expanded. Now roughly 40 percent of the population engage in farming and about the same percentage in industry. Industrialization, however, was accompanied by complicated phenomena of social transformation, notably the explosive growth of the urban population associated with massive migration from rural areas, an expanding number of industrial workers, and a growing polarization of wealth between rich and poor. Matters regulating economic activities, such as antipollution measures, zoning, regulations related to drugs, food, clothing, public health in general, safety in building construction, firearms, explosives, and many other concerns have emerged as pressing legal problems. Politically the most serious problems facing Korea are those of distribution of wealth and of participation to be solved without slowing down economic growth. Of legal interest are labor law, the realization of the constitutionally envisioned social justice, and the welfare state. As in other fields of law, the constitution established not only full-fledged labor rights but also labor laws. These are among the most advanced labor laws in the world, because the Korean labor law was enacted after the model of the most advanced Western labor laws, those of the United States, Germany, and Japan. Initially, the Korean labor law lacked the industrial base to meet its requirements. Now with economic growth, the needed industrial base emerged but is still not sufficient to keep pace with the rapid economic growth while meeting growing labor demands under the present predatory world economic conditions. Korea is poorly endowed with natural resources.

The oil shock of 1973 and 1978 was a blow to the Korean economy. From the perspective of foreign investors, Korea was initially (and still is) a risk area where war could break out at any time. Cheap and docile labor as well as tax benefits and other incentives have to be offered to attract foreign investors. Consequently, the rights of workers in foreign firms were curtailed in favor of these investors. As part of emergency measures, brought about by the growing North Korean threat and the prospect of American military withdrawal, labor rights since 1971 have been placed under various industry-wide restrictions. Along with labor demands, there are growing demands for the expansion of welfare programs, which at present are still in their starting stage. The constitutionally spelled out legal ideals are far ahead of Korean reality; they are more in line with those of socioeconomically more advanced Western societies. They state the goals but their very statement aggravates the mass frustration. With industrialization wealth has been concentrated in large urban centers. Now urban capital has begun also to be invested in rural areas, bringing up still cheap farmlands, not for productive, but for commercially profitable purposes. There is an outcry that absentee landlords have quietly begun to reestablish themselves. And abolition of the maximum limit on farmland holding for promotion of farming enterprises and mechanization of agriculture is now being debated. Recently accumulated capital generally drove up the price of land. The issue of state control of land use is a focal point of discussion today.

Law plays a special role in industrial growth and related social transformation. The political leadership of the government thus far played a greater role in inducing industrialization than anything else in Korea by way of wooing foreign loans and investments. The role of law has been regulatory rather than formative. In Korean industrialization, law has been a variable dependent on political, economic, and social factors. Moreover, legal structure and process remain relatively unchanged in their relationships to the over-all social structure and processes. Lawyers made few contributions to industrialization. Indications of potentially significant changes in legal structure and process that have recently appeared on the Korean social scene are related to the sudden demands for more lawyer specialists in international trade.

SUMMARY

The law of the Yi dynasty was an exercise of *imperium*, lacking the principles and rules of law designed to restrain the ruler. It was, however, interwoven with a system of positive moral principles which applied to the ruler. The moral system designed to curb the ruler's arbitrary use of power was Confucianism.

The law of Korea under Japanese rule was in its forms Western. But it lacked both public law and a system of positive moral principles: it was despotic law designed to rule the colonized.

The present formal law of Korea has three elements: the law reflecting the power relationship between the ruler and the ruled, public law designed to subject the ruler to the rules of law, and the law governing relationships between private parties. In a modern democratic polity, the second element is more important with the rising expectation of the masses for political participation. As seen by Koreans, however, the three elements of the present law are of Western origin. The second element, public law, is accompanied by a serious issue of indigenization. The problems include the considerations of which political, social, and economic conditions for social change are needed for public law to take root in Korea. A serious problem facing Korea today stems at least partly from the fact that the Confucian equivalent of public law lost its previous vigor and institutional support, while public law has not fully been indigenized.

The formal rational quality is also under strain. In terms of "living" law, the present legal system is not relevant to many of the political, social, and cultural processes in Korea. And yet liberal values, instilled by liberal education, the presence of intellectuals, the emergence of a middle class, the presence of a legal profession, and economic prosperity, are positive extra-legal factors conducive to the realization of liberal democracy in Korea. There are also growing signs of constitutionalism.

A vision of Korea as a unified, democratic, and industrialized nation-state has been positing itself as the overarching goal and as a serious challenge to Korea and to its legal system. The international environment and the presence of North Korea, however, render early fulfillment of the goal of national unification unrealistic. The constitution envisions a united Korea, but realistically two Koreas are the best alternative at present, with South Korea, one may hope, commanding economic and cultural superiority, like West Germany vis-à-vis East Germany. Precarious international peace depending on a complicated balance of power among big powers surrounding Korea, the threat from North Korea, and the aspiration for national unification are real and potential extralegal factors that tend to retard the realization of a full-fledged democracy. South Korean survival as a liberal democracy is at stake. An external threat to the survival of a liberal system poses itself as a serious challenge to its constitutional order even in a society where democracy is long established. Thus, there emerges the paradox of liberal democratic values working against liberal democratic values.

The goals of liberal democracy and industrialization within the framework of a market economy have equally been conditioned by historical and environmental factors and by domestic variables including a constitutional factor prescribing a full-fledged liberal and social democratic nation in which social justice is realized. The strong need for industrialization—a nationalist aspiration—against a backdrop of lack of capital, skilled personnel, and raw materials, and the political-social consequences of industrialization—explosive urbanization, polarization of the rich and poor, and the growing political consciousness of the lower classes—are also among the major factors that militate against democracy. Whether political democracy and economic development can be realized in a few decades while meeting the expectations of the population for a high level of democratic performance and delivery of economic prosperity is a thorny question. The historical evidence seems to project a negative picture, namely that democracy usually comes at the expense of prosperity and vice versa, for a late comer. Especially, rapid economic development comes at the expense of democratic development; the former is attained under strong governmental leadership, as shown in Japan and Soviet Russia.[88] Besides, not only advanced Western countries, but even Japan and Russia had many advantages over the latecomers after the Second

[88] Cyril E. Black et al., *The Modernization of Japan and Russia: A Comparative Study* (New York: Free Press, 1975).

World War. Japan did not have to meet such strong democratic expectations of the population in their initial stage as in a non-Communist Third World country as Korea today. Soviet Russia is armed with a Communist ideology, which not only justifies but glorifies totalitarian governmental control. As for Western countries, political revolution, industrialization, general franchise, and the welfare state all came one after another in a leisurely pace. But in a Third World country all these critical stages came at the same time following the world-wide democratic trend after the Second World War. In the recent rapid economic growth, government leadership played a pronounced role while maintaining a liberal democratic constitutional order and a market-economy framework, and without resorting to totalitarian government control or being reduced to state capitalism. In the process, liberal democratic aspirations were not fully met at their advanced level as in the Western countries. Another problem confronting Korea is that of meeting growing popular expectations for a larger share of economic wealth produced by recent industrialization without endangering capital accumulation needed for sustained economic growth. The issue is related to the problem of how to internalize the rule of law and to increase its role in governmental and social processes, and the problem of how to realize social justice.

The last point of concern refers to cultural factors. Whatever the broad framework may have been, small-group social structures and cultural patterns remain very much traditional Korean. In the over-all social processes, law still plays a relatively minor role, as compared with that in a Western society. Law is still assigned a criminal, regulatory, and retributory role rather than a means of justice. In settling conflicts and disputes, conciliatory ways still prevail. An authoritarian social structure and a lack of a democratic tradition are characteristic. Such a legal culture will not likely give way to Western ways in the near future. To that extent, Western concepts and notions of law along with Western legal institutions and jurisprudence do not apply to Korean society. No cultural eccentricism is espoused here. Copying Western jurisprudence alone will not solve Korea's problems. In formulating Korea's legal solutions, consideration must be given not only to particular political, social, and economic problems but also to cultural patterns. For example, the legal profession played a small role in recent industrialization, contrary to a role that Western legal scholars might naïvely assign to them. A greater demand for special legal service began to emerge only during the past few years in international transactions following industrialization and expanded foreign trade. Many problems related to the legal profession, including recruitment, training, ethical standards, and disciplinary questions are still conceived predominantly as matters of public concern rather than concerns of the bar. Because of a legacy of a few nationalist lawyers who fought the Japanese on behalf of nationalist defendants without financial consideration and as part of upper-class culture, the practice of lawyers of accepting financial rewards for their services is looked upon with ambivalence in the popular image of lawyers. The image of a licensed thief is accepted in Korean culture. Lawyers are still employed largely as last resorts, mostly for court-room performance and much less for preventive and preparatory reasons, such as drawing up deeds, wills, and contracts, and counseling for broader social processes. What the future holds for the role of law in Korean society is uncertain, but a careful reading of its historical development is surely the first step to answering this query.

Professor Dai-Kwon Choi is currently Assistant Professor at the Law School, Seoul National University. He completed his work for the Ph.D. degree at the University of California, Berkeley, and his Ph.D. dissertation entitled "Law and Social Change: The Korean Experience" is in the process of being revised for publication. He spent the academic year 1979–80 at Berkeley as a visiting scholar and is the author of several articles on Korean law.